**New Directions for Child and Adolescent Development**

Lene Arnett Jensen
Reed W. Larson
EDITORS-IN-CHIEF

William Damon
FOUNDING EDITOR

# Pathways to Adulthood for Disconnected Young Men in Low-Income Communities

Kevin Roy
Nikki Jones
EDITORS

Number 143 • Spring 2014
Jossey-Bass
San Francisco

Λ

PATHWAYS TO ADULTHOOD FOR DISCONNECTED YOUNG MEN IN LOW-INCOME
COMMUNITIES
*Kevin Roy, Nikki Jones* (eds.)
New Directions for Child and Adolescent Development, no. 143
*Lene Arnett Jensen, Reed W. Larson,* Editors-in-Chief

Microfilm copies of issues and articles are available in 16 mm and 35 mm,
as well as microfiche in 105 mm, through University Microfilms, Inc., 300
North Zeeb Road, Ann Arbor, Michigan 48106-1346.

ISSN 1520-3247    electronic ISSN 1534-8687

NEW DIRECTIONS FOR CHILD AND ADOLESCENT DEVELOPMENT is part of The
Jossey-Bass Education Series and is published quarterly by Wiley
Subscription Services, Inc., a Wiley company, at Jossey-Bass, One
Montgomery Street, Suite 1200, San Francisco, CA 94104-4594. Post-
master: Send address changes to New Directions for Child and Adoles-
cent Development, Jossey-Bass, One Montgomery Street, Suite 1200, San
Francisco, CA 94104-4594.

*New Directions for Child and Adolescent Development* is indexed in Cam-
bridge Scientific Abstracts (CSA/CIG), CHID: Combined Health Informa-
tion Database (NIH), Contents Pages in Education (T&F), Educational
Research Abstracts Online (T&F), Embase (Elsevier), ERIC Database
(Education Resources Information Center), Index Medicus/MEDLINE
(NLM), Linguistics & Language Behavior Abstracts (CSA/CIG), Psycho-
logical Abstracts/PsycINFO (APA), Social Services Abstracts (CSA/CIG),
SocINDEX (EBSCO), and Sociological Abstracts (CSA/CIG).

INDIVIDUAL SUBSCRIPTION RATE (in USD): $89 per year US/Can/Mex,
$113 rest of world; institutional subscription rate: $388 US, $428
Can/Mex, $462 rest of world. Single copy rate: $29. Electronic only–all
regions: $89 individual, $388 institutional; Print & Electronic–US: $98
individual, $450 institutional; Print & Electronic–Canada/Mexico:
$98 individual, $490 institutional; Print & Electronic–Rest of World:
$122 individual, $524 institutional.

EDITORIAL CORRESPONDENCE should be e-mailed to the editors-in-chief:
Lene Arnett Jensen (ljensen@clarku.edu) and Reed W. Larson (larsonr@
illinois.edu).

Jossey-Bass Web address: www.josseybass.com

# CONTENTS

Roy, K., & Jones, N. (2014). Theorizing alternative pathways through adulthood: Unequal social arrangements in the lives of young disadvantaged men. In K. Roy & N. Jones (Eds.), *Pathways to adulthood for disconnected young men in low-income communities. New Directions in Child and Adolescent Development, 143*, 1–9.

1

# Theorizing Alternative Pathways Through Adulthood: Unequal Social Arrangements in the Lives of Young Disadvantaged Men

*Kevin Roy, Nikki Jones*

## Abstract

*This chapter introduces the innovative field-based studies on disadvantaged men that are featured in this volume. Together, these studies of disadvantaged men from diverse racial and ethnic backgrounds and both urban and nonurban settings complement and extend recent discussions of emerging adulthood, which typically conceptualizes the transition to adulthood as a normative and linear process. The authors offer that the research presented here provides a more accurate rendering of the transition to adulthood for young disadvantaged men. For disadvantaged young men, the transition to adulthood is often complex and nonlinear, and features a diversity of pathways that are often overlooked in contemporary research on transitions to adulthood. The chapter ends with a call for research and theory that better reflects the precarious nature of pathways to adulthood for disadvantaged men in urban and nonurban settings. Researchers are encouraged to draw on findings from field-based studies to inform policies and practices directed at minimizing the marginalization of disadvantaged men from mainstream society. © 2014 Wiley Periodicals, Inc.*

> For young people from the upper-middle class, whose parents can afford to bankroll them while they experiment with careers, relationships and identities, the period between adolescence and adulthood may in fact be an odyssey.... But poor inner-city and rural youth, as well as young people who live in the so-called red states, are far less likely than their advantaged, suburban and blue-state counterparts to delay the transition into conventional work and family roles, both because they choose not to and because they simply can't afford to.
>
> > Steinberg (2007, para. 1–2)

The fates of young men have diverged dramatically since the 1970s, in large part due to changes in global and local economies (Sum, Khatiwada, McLaughlin, & Palma, 2011). For men with resources, the transition into adulthood is synonymous with experimentation with autonomy and self-exploration, risks and excesses (Kimmel, 2008; Twenge, 2006), and often greater educational opportunities and more freedom in personal and professional choices than previous decades (Arnett & Tanner, 2005; Settersten, Furstenberg, & Rumbaut, 2005; Settersten & Ray, 2010). Due to the extreme inequalities in contemporary U.S. society, however, young men without resources often lose ground over this developmental period. They are challenged to complete a high school education, which has increased worth in a global economy. They face disproportionately higher odds of incarceration. They confront critical challenges from law enforcement and courts, peers in street life, skeptical family members, and expectant partners with children in need of resources. Young men in low-income neighborhoods are uniquely vulnerable during the transition to adulthood, and we remain challenged to understand and to alter the marginalization of these men.

In this volume, we present innovative research focused on the contexts, processes, and meanings in life pathways for disadvantaged young men as they move from adolescence into adulthood. In many ways, this collection of studies was inspired by an earlier collection of research on the experiences of young urban girls of color (Leadbetter & Way, 1996). The papers in this volume highlight how traditional gender expectations, including rigid understandings of manhood and masculinity, shape the experiences of young disadvantaged men as they transition into adulthood. Adolescent boys of color who come of age in disadvantaged urban neighborhoods, for example, are often called upon to manage adult relationships and responsibilities at early ages. Whether they are pressured to be a so-called real man on the street or a "man of the house" at home, this process of adultification can feel overwhelming and, at times, can lead young men to retreat from the responsibilities and obligations typically associated with manhood as they enter their late-teens and early twenties. For some, meeting the gendered expectations embedded in understandings of what it means to be a good provider or a good father can give new meaning to their lives, which can shore men up as they transition to adulthood. The economic uncertainty that characterizes their lives, however, can present a challenge to these efforts, leaving some men feeling as if they have fallen short of their efforts to be good men, husbands, or fathers. Utilizing extensive field-based data on hard-to-reach populations of young adult men, our goals are to encourage conceptualization and theory development for the transition to adulthood for disadvantaged young men from diverse racial and ethnic backgrounds, and to shape hypotheses on how youth strategize for stability despite dramatic changes in their lives over time.

## Inequality and the Model of Emerging Adulthood

The chapters in this volume emerged from a panel presentation at the Society for Research on Adolescence in March 2010. We realized from the outset that our research collectively reflected a very different side of the emerging adulthood debate that had begun to play a prominent role in understanding the lives of young adults (Arnett, 2004). While we share some common focus with the emerging adulthood framework, we want to expand the dialogue across disciplines, across methods, and most significantly across social and historical contexts. The stage model of emerging adulthood is embedded with certain assumptions about young adults' linear and almost inevitable forward motion, their progress toward successful adult outcomes and role fulfillment. Our work problematizes the measurement of social class as a variable and offers insight into the consequences of exclusion in an era of rising and unprecedented inequality. These chapters contribute to an understanding of the complex social location of young, economically disadvantaged men of color that is often lacking in intersectional approaches (Dill & Zambrana, 2009).

Arnett and colleagues argue that emerging adulthood is a developmentally distinct stage of life, a new period that is defined by age and is universal across social contexts. However, the contours of this proposed stage shift dramatically for the groups of young men who we address in these four chapters. We find that they do not move through the challenges of young adulthood in sync with their peers who attend college, who choose internships to build social capital, or who plan for the right time to get married or to have children. These young men negotiate these challenges throughout the course of their lives—some still struggling to settle down at age of 40 or 50 and others coping with adultification and exposure to adult responsibilities at very young ages (Burton, 2007).

Creation of one's own identity does remain a central task for young men in our studies. Erikson, and Arnett after him, argues that this reflects a specific stage in life. However, we link the efforts of young "men of the house," of men who confront the threat of violence and targeted police surveillance in their home communities, and of young migrant laborers who are confused as to how to be fathers to their children, not to age-specific tasks but to unequal social arrangements with context-defining institutions, such as the incarceration industry, limited local economies, struggling families, and attenuated education systems. As with other youth in a globalized world, these men must craft a working biography of their own selves; they must individualize their experiences in the midst of growing inequality and dwindling resources to remake themselves again and again (Beck & Beck-Gernsheim, 2002).

## Unequal Social Arrangements Through Mass Incarceration

Perhaps the most consequential new social arrangement to emerge over the last 40 years is the rise of mass incarceration. In *Punishment and Inequality in America*, sociologist and demographer Bruce Western writes that the "penal system is now an important part of an American system of social stratification" (Western, 2006, p. 12). His analysis reveals that the negative consequences of this new system reshape the life course of entire demographic groups, especially poor Black and Hispanic men with little schooling. Today, prison and its associated apparatus (e.g., zero-tolerance policies in schools, the intersection of the criminal justice and health care systems, and the embrace of targeted enforcement programs like "stop-and-frisk" in New York City) is a "major institutional presence" in the lives of disadvantaged young men like those described in the chapters from Richardson and Jones. In contrast to adolescent boys who come of age in more stable, middle-class settings, the young men featured in these two chapters and those who care for them must learn to manage a three-pronged threat to their well-being: the threat of lethal violence, which remains at chronic levels in some settings even in the wake of the Great Crime Decline; routine exposure to targeted police surveillance; and the pull of formal and informal ties to the criminal justice system.

As Richardson explains, the parents and caretakers of Black adolescent boys coming of age in tough urban neighborhoods confront a dilemma: keep children close to home or keep them safe? How parents resolve such dilemmas is often contingent on social capital, which varies across and within neighborhoods. For those parents who are most precariously positioned in the neighborhood, institutional exile—effectively giving up a young man to the juvenile justice system—comes to make sense as a parenting strategy. While this strategy may help to keep young people alive in the short term, it also leads to the accumulation of negative social capital. This is just one of the ways that the shift toward mass incarceration encourages a set of situated practices that exacerbate inequality and are likely to have serious consequences for young people's successful transitions to adulthood.

Young men left behind in distressed urban neighborhoods must contend with a contradictory set of challenges that is shaped by their social circumstances: they remain routine targets for lethal violence and police surveillance. Young, Black men like the ones described in the chapters from

NEW DIRECTIONS FOR CHILD AND ADOLESCENT DEVELOPMENT • DOI: 10.1002/cad

Richardson and Jones are often seen as threats (Anderson, 2011; Jones & Jackson, 2011), and little attention is given to how routine interactions with the police might influence their social development. The degree to which the life space of poor, urban young Black men has been altered in the mass incarceration era is aptly illustrated in Jones's ethnographic account of how young men become socialized into the stop-and-frisk and other types of routine encounters with the police that were described as "the regular routine" by one of her respondents. Her study reveals how routine encounters with the police are best understood as *a set of patterned social interactions that structure the daily lives of young men* in high-surveillance neighborhoods. Jones's chapter encourages us to consider the consequences of this sort of socialization for healthy adolescent development. Together, these two chapters suggest that instead of an emerging adulthood, poor, urban young men of color, especially those with ties to the criminal justice system, are more likely to experience an *arrested adulthood* as threats of lethal violence and frequent encounters with law enforcement interrupt the forward progress that is often associated with positive adolescent development and successful transitions to adulthood.

## Unequal Social Arrangements in Postfamilial Families

The "postfamilial" family marks unknown territory for many young adults. It is unclear who parents should "be" to their adult sons, and how they should support them in a protracted transition to adulthood. They may provide a sense of belonging and embeddedness that is distinct from childhood and adolescence, and offer supports as adult children navigate uncertain pathways to school and work (Furlong & Cartmel, 2007). The model of emerging adulthood reflects the process of concerted cultivation in Annette Lareau's (2003) research on unequal childhood and divergent parenting practices across race and class. Families may face many years of exploration and uncertainty, but they invest intensive amounts of concentrated resources in their children to ensure success. In long years of support for college, or a down payment on a first home or apartment, adult sons are recipients of these resources. In this way, some families live up to the ideal of becoming launching pads for successful young adults.

For many young disadvantaged men, however, families present complicated relationships that shift and transform in early adult years. Young men develop long-term relationships with parents, siblings, and extended kin that do not fade out with a launch into adulthood. Obligations in families with limited resources continue and may increase in a transition to adulthood. Similar to Lareau's (2003) notion of natural growth, parents may play a less central role in their sons' growth. Obligations flow both ways: families share extensive but diffused resources, and sons are contributors just as frequently as their parents or other family members.

When families need their adult sons' time and money to survive on a daily basis, the transition to adulthood is transformed. In his study of two urban communities in Maryland, Roy explores how young men managed households for their mothers for many years, caring for children and delegating household tasks and space. They also contributed money through illegal activities that put them at great risk for incarceration, injury, and trauma. For some, these adult-like responsibilities ended abruptly during adolescence, with the entry of stepfathers and mothers' boyfriends into their households. Pushed out of the role of "man of the house," young men in economically disadvantaged families struggled to regain authority and esteem. Some isolated themselves from family members and friends, in an effort to figure out how to become self-sufficient with few opportunities for school and work. This ethnographic finding illustrates a crisis of connection in early adulthood that Way (2011) identifies for many of the same adolescents in poor urban communities.

Young men are considered adults within their kin networks, and their attempts to find work, finish school, or start a family can lead to self-sufficiency which is a gift and a threat to family members. Settersten's research examines how young men struggle to adapt with off-time transitions. He and his colleagues argue that for many disadvantaged men, early fatherhood can facilitate other markers of adulthood, such as employment. For the Latino fathers in Oregon in his study, these unexpected turning points in family life were full of risk but also gave men new opportunities to reframe their past experiences—and new motivation to find an adequate context for raising children and becoming adults, even with low-wage work and limited educational options.

## Unequal Social Arrangements as Process of Disconnection

These four chapters problematize many of the assumptions that support a model of emerging adulthood for young men who experience varying degrees of disconnection and disadvantage. For example, as a young disadvantaged man enters the status of being "disconnected," his lack of participation in school and work is often framed as a personal problem, the solution to which is a matter of personal change. Becoming a successful adult is framed as a matter of appropriate choices. With the acquisition of the appropriate skills for a good job, he can "connect." By avoiding risky behavior, he can remain "connected." Social policy and interventions are focused, as a result, on linking disconnected, disadvantaged young men with job training, job placement, and spots in community colleges, vocational training, and even colleges and universities.

These chapters demonstrate, however, that lack of participation in school and work is a result of long-term processes of disconnection that were set in motion before personal decisions are often made. The young men in these studies have adapted to *being at risk* in their homes and communities, and to *being a risk* to those in those same locations, at times through no direct action of their own. Through adultification, they learned to support their families as many adults would. For these young men, becoming an adult is less a matter of choice—of a school, a job, or a relationship—but a matter of survival, of getting by with few options (Silva, 2013). In some ways, we might question whether a "transition" to adulthood actually takes place, when young men take on serious adult-like risks and responsibilities as boys or adolescents.

As we stress, there are few secure pathways for young disadvantaged men. Instead, new institutions have developed as holding zones, such as mass incarceration, permanently marginalized sections of the job market, or even programs that allow nonresidential unwed fathers limited involvement with their children. If we examine these institutions and their relations with young men closely, our focus turns from promotion of individual change toward changing institutions in ways that will support successful transitions to adulthood for a broader swath of youth (Bynner, 2005). Which systems serve to exclude young disadvantaged men from successful markers of adulthood, and which systems might support inclusion and investment as alternatives?

## A Call for Theorizing Transitions Among Diverse Groups of Young Men

Finally, this volume should be read as a call to encourage new ways to conceptualize transitions to adulthood for young, disadvantaged men. In each of these chapters, we demonstrate the limitations of the emerging adulthood model to provide concepts that fit with the life experiences of the men in this volume. When we typically conceptualize transitions, we assume some to be failed transitions and others to be successful, such as finding a good job or earning a college degree. The transition to adulthood from a developmental perspective is normative and linear. What our research suggests, in contrast, is that transition to adulthood is complex and nonlinear, featuring a diversity of pathways, moving in fits and starts, forward and backward. Even young men are unable to shed past experiences and labels—such as ex-offender or dropout—and their success as an adult is held in doubt.

Instead, the years of transition are periods of active negotiation, as these men attempt to restore order to the complexity in their lives (Furlong & Cartmel, 2007; Osgood, Foster, Flanagan, & Ruth, 2005). They learn to live with uncertainty and to build stable identities marked by economic and social marginality. They transform roles as fathers, workers, friends, and sons and adapt to very real challenges in their day-to-day routines, all while perhaps making little progress toward normative goals. These "successful" outcomes appear to be out of sync with the complicated risks that many young adult men face in their households, their neighborhoods, and in their larger communities.

For young disadvantaged men, the negotiation of school, work, family life, parenthood, and other markers of adulthood may start earlier and stretch out over a long period of time, perhaps even longer than for young adults who do not experience adultification or disconnection. Although a transition is protracted, it still remains unequal: some young adults will settle into "success" and others will fall even further behind, beginning a pileup of many years of cumulative disadvantage (DiPrete & Eirich, 2006). Persistent inequality has produced divergent experiences that are not adequately captured by the concept of emerging adulthood. A variety of new social arrangements have taken a toll on young, disadvantaged men. Our conceptual model of making a successful transition to adulthood should account for the experiences of this group of young men.

## References

Anderson, E. (2011). Toward knowing the iconic ghetto. In R. Hutchison & B. D. Haynes (Eds.), *The ghetto: Contemporary global issues and controversies* (pp. 67–82). Boulder, CO: Westview Press.

Arnett, J. (2004). *Emerging adulthood: The winding road from late teens through the twenties*. New York, NY: Oxford University Press.

Arnett, J., & Tanner, J. (2005). *Emerging adults in America: Coming of age in the 21st century*. Washington, DC: American Psychological Association Press.

Beck, U., & Beck-Gernsheim, E. (2002). *Individualization: Institutionalized individualism and its social and political consequences*. Thousand Oaks, CA: Sage.

Burton, L. (2007). Childhood adultification in economically disadvantaged families: A conceptual model. *Family Relations, 56,* 329–345.

Bynner, J. (2005). Rethinking the youth phase of the life course: The case for emerging adulthood? *Journal of Youth Studies, 8,* 367–384.

Dill, B. T., & Zambrana, R. (Eds.). (2009). *Emerging intersections: Race, class, and gender in theory, policy and practice*. New York, NY: Rutgers University Press.

DiPrete, T. A., & Eirich, G. M. (2006). Cumulative advantage as a mechanism for inequality: A review of theoretical and empirical developments. *Annual Review of Sociology, 32,* 271–297.

Furlong, A., & Cartmel, F. (2007). *Young people and social change: New perspectives*. New York, NY: Open University Press.

Jones, N., & Jackson, C. (2011). "You just don't go down there": Learning to avoid the ghetto in San Francisco. In R. Hutchison & B. D. Haynes (Eds.), *The ghetto: Contemporary global issues and controversies* (pp. 83–110). Boulder, CO: Westview Press.

Kimmel, M. (2008). *Guyland: The perilous world where boys become men*. New York, NY: Harper Collins.

Lareau, A. (2003). *Unequal childhoods: Class, race, and family life*. Berkeley, CA: University of California Press.

Leadbetter, B., & Way, N. (1996). *Urban girls: Resisting stereotypes, creating identities*. New York, NY: New York University Press.

Osgood, W., Foster, E. M., Flanagan, C., & Ruth, G. (Eds.). (2005). *On your own without a net: The transition to adulthood for vulnerable populations*. Chicago, IL: University of Chicago Press.

Settersten, R., Furstenberg, F., & Rumbaut, R. (Eds.). (2005). *On the frontier of adulthood: Theory, research, and public policy*. Chicago, IL: University of Chicago Press.

Settersten, R., & Ray, B. (2010). *Not quite adults: Why 20-somethings are choosing a slower path to adulthood, and why it's good for everyone*. New York, NY: Bantam.

Silva, J. (2013). *Coming up short: Working-class adulthood in an age of uncertainty*. New York, NY: Oxford University Press.

Steinberg, L. (2007, October 11). The "I'm Just Finding Myself" Decade—Letter. *The New York Times*. http://www.nytimes.com/2007/10/11/opinion/11odyssey.html

Sum, A., Khatiwada, I., McLaughlin, J., & Palma, S. (2011). No country for young men: Deteriorating labor market prospects for low-skilled men in the United States. *Annals of the American Academy of Political and Social Science, 635*, 24–55.

Twenge, J. (2006). *Generation me: Why today's young Americans are more confident, assertive, entitled—and more miserable than ever before*. New York, NY: Free Press.

Way, N. (2011). *Deep secrets: Boys' friendships and the crisis of connection*. Cambridge, MA: Harvard University Press

Western, B. (2006). *Punishment and inequality in America*. New York, NY: Russell Sage Foundation.

KEVIN ROY *is an associate professor in the Department of Family Science, School of Public Health at the University of Maryland, College Park. E-mail: kroy@umd.edu, webpage: http://www.sph.umd.edu/fmsc/people/fac/kroy.html*

NIKKI JONES *is an associate professor of African American studies at the University of California, Berkeley. E-mail: njones@berkeley.edu, webpage: betweengoodandghetto.com*

Richardson, J. B., Jr., Van Brakle, M., & St. Vil, C. (2014). Taking boys out of the hood: Exile as a parenting strategy for African American male youth. In K. Roy & N. Jones (Eds.), *Pathways to adulthood for disconnected young men in low-income communities. New Directions for Child and Adolescent Development, 143*, 11–31.

# 2

# Taking Boys Out of the Hood: Exile as a Parenting Strategy for African American Male Youth

*Joseph B. Richardson, Jr., Mischelle Van Brakle, Christopher St. Vil*

## Abstract

*Research indicates that inner-city neighborhood effects are correlated with school dropout, substance abuse, crime, violence, homicide, HIV risk related behaviors, and incarceration for adolescent African American males. Parents of adolescent African American males face many challenges as they try to keep their children safe in high-risk neighborhoods. Parents often use multiple parenting approaches to improve the life chances and opportunities for this vulnerable population of youth. This chapter elaborates on the concept of exile. Exile is a parenting strategy used by parents to relocate young African American males living in high-risk communities to safer spaces. Drawing on qualitative data collected from a longitudinal ethnographic research study on the social context of adolescent violence among African American males, this chapter examines exile as a parenting approach used to keep children safe. © 2014 Wiley Periodicals, Inc.*

---

*Note:* All coauthors are in agreement with the content of this chapter, and the present study was conducted in accordance with the ethical standards of the American Psychological Association. The findings reported in this chapter have not been previously published nor is the chapter being simultaneously submitted elsewhere.

M any parents living in neighborhoods marked by poverty and crime do not have the financial means to select neighborhoods that are safe. These parents often adopt other management strategies to shield their children from local dangers and connect them to sources of human and social capital. Studies have demonstrated how parents reduce risk and create opportunities for their adolescent children despite living in impoverished communities marked by neighborhood decay, crime, overcrowded schools, and limited resources (Brooks-Gunn, Duncan, & Aber, 1997; Furstenberg, 2000; Jarrett, 1995, 1999). Some of these strategies include strict supervision of youth through curfews, chaperonage, discouraging friendships with delinquent peers, and seeking resources within and beyond the community. Parents also utilize kinship networks of grandparents, older siblings, godparents, and other biological and fictive kin who can provide broader opportunities for youths (Jarrett, 1997, 1999). This chapter examines another common parenting approach: exile. This strategy is commonly used by parents of African American males who are especially concerned with protecting adolescent boys from threats of physical violence.

## Neighborhood Context, Violence, and Young Black Men

Exposure to community violence is disproportionately higher among the poor, people of color, and those who live in densely populated urban areas (Sampson, Raudenbush, & Earls, 1997). Youth living within disadvantaged communities are at higher risk of being exposed to violence and also experience fewer opportunities for positive relationships and prosocial models than other populations of youth (Brooks-Gunn et al., 1997; Lynch & Cicchetti, 2002). Research reveals that adolescents, particularly poor African American adolescents, are at higher risk for exposure to community violence than youth of other racial and age groups (Voisin, 2007). Exposure to community violence also significantly contributes to the morbidity and mortality of African American male adolescents and young adults (Cooper, Eslinger, Nash, Al Zawahri, & Stolley, 2000; Cooper, Eslinger, & Stolley, 2006; Prothrow-Stith, 1991; Rich & Grey, 2005).

Homicide is the leading cause of death for African American men between the ages of 15 and 34 (CDC, 2013). In a study of early violent deaths among juvenile offenders, Black males were four times more likely than the general population of youth to die from a violent firearm injury (Teplin, McClelland, Abram, & Mileusnic, 2005). Anderson (1999) suggests that there is an informal code in many inner-city communities that directs social behavior and norms among young African American men. The code, which, as Anderson explains, is a by-product of an oppositional culture created by inner-city Black males in response to the lack of faith in the police and the criminal justice system, governs interpersonal violence and behavior among young Black men where respect is a highly valued commodity and used as a

NEW DIRECTIONS FOR CHILD AND ADOLESCENT DEVELOPMENT • DOI: 10.1002/cad

form of social capital in communities often deplete of resources. Inner-city neighborhoods provide limited economic, institutional and social resources for the families and adolescents living there. In the absence of basic assets, "the streets" in impoverished communities become the major lifestyle contender and developmental niche for many young people. In the ghetto street culture, respect is a form of social capital that substitutes for other absent forms of capital (Anderson, 1999; Jarrett, 1999).

Since respect is a highly valued commodity in these settings, being disrespected (or being dissed) often results in retaliatory violence. Disadvantaged youth who hold beliefs that are consistent with the code of the street are significantly more likely to engage in violence (Brezina, Agnew, Cullen, & Wright, 2004). One study of violence and trauma among young Black men in Baltimore City revealed that "disrespect" or "being dissed" was described as the cause of a violent injury in 81% of violent events among Black male participants in a hospital-based violence intervention program (Cooper et al., 2000). In order for young Black men to stay safe in high-risk neighborhoods, they must abide by the code regardless of whether they subscribe to its principles or not. Although research indicates that these factors may be predictive of higher rates of violent victimization among adolescent Black males, we know little about the strategies parents use to ensure the physical safety of young Black males living in high-risk neighborhoods.

## Parenting Strategies in High-Risk Neighborhoods

Parents in poor inner-city communities often struggle to create protective resilient factors that will enhance their children's individual coping abilities. Their hope is that these factors will, in turn, decrease their vulnerability to negative outcomes.[1] Protective factors fall into three major categories: (a) personal attributes of the individual, (b) affectional ties within the family, and (c) existence of external support systems which arise at school or within the community.

The ability of poor parents to tap into external systems of support to create protective factors for their children significantly depends on the levels of social capital parents possess. The social capital they possess provides them with the opportunity to take full advantage of the information channels, trustworthiness, and sense of mutual obligation inherent in the social relationships that can promote successful adolescent development.[2] Despite limited resources in these communities, parents who are socially integrated into local communities are often better able to command social capital and locate the limited higher quality resources that prevent delinquency (Furstenberg, 2000; Jarrett, 1995, 1997). Families without access to social capital are often left on their own to parent in difficult circumstances, and the outcomes are often negative.[3] In the present study, we use qualitative data to examine a parenting strategy that we describe as *exile*: the process of removing children from distressed neighborhoods to safe spaces outside the community in which they reside. This strategy is often employed by low-income parents and families with both high and low levels of social capital.

## Qualitative Research on Parenting Strategies

Qualitative accounts of poor African American families and youth illuminate strategies that parents create to combat the deleterious effects of living in an inner-city neighborhood. Jarrett's (1997, 1999) qualitative work examines how African American families in impoverished neighborhoods promote social mobility among adolescents and discourage delinquency. These parenting strategies include family protection strategies, child monitoring strategies, parental resource-seeking strategies, and in-home learning strategies. For parents living in high-risk neighborhoods, seeking out and identifying resources that exist outside of the community for their children is critical in combating the high-risk factors associated with inner-city residence. Jarrett (1997) described the strategy of seeking protective resources outside of the local community as a community-bridging strategy. This strategy has the potential to connect disadvantaged youth to social and cultural capital that exists outside of the community. More importantly, community-bridging strategies have the potential to protect the physical safety of inner-city youth, shielding them from neighborhood influences by closely supervising time, space, and peer relationships.

In her study of African American parenting in low-income neighborhoods, Jarrett (1997) noted that when monitoring strategies such as intensive supervision and chaperonage become ineffective, parents resorted to extreme measures. The strategy of "exile" is viewed as one type of extreme measure that some parents may employ when traditional parenting strategies prove ineffective.

Exile is a community-bridging parenting strategy used by poor African American parents to keep children safe by connecting youth to extra-local resources. For parents living in northern urban cities such as the parents in this study, these variations include parents who sent their children to live permanently with relatives in the rural South as a strategy for keeping them safe. Historically, in many poor African American families from the rural South who migrated to northern cities, parents often sent their children to the South to live with extended family members to keep them safe and to avoid the negative effects associated with living in impoverished inner-city neighborhoods (Brown, 1965).

In this chapter, we expand upon Jarrett's concept by identifying and describing three types of exile observed in this study: temporary exile, permanent exile, and institutional exile. Temporary forms of exile are characterized by periods when parents send their children away for short durations of time. Examples of temporary forms of exile include parents sending children to stay with relatives on the weekends or summers outside of the local community. Permanent exile is a more extreme form of exile used by parents with few resources to protect their children. Permanent exile involves parents sending children to stay with relatives or other significant adults for an indefinite period of time. This form of exile is usually accompanied by school enrollment at the exiled location. Often, parents used temporary exile and permanent exile in concert, depending on the situation and circumstances of their children. An extreme form of permanent exile is institutional exile, where parents rely on the juvenile justice system to provide at-risk youth a safe haven from the streets. For these parents, the security of juvenile detention is considered to be a protective factor from neighborhood violence. Parents with greater social capital may be less likely to rely on exile as a strategy because they possess strong informal networks that they can use to provide protective factors for their children. Parents that possess greater levels of social capital in resource-deprived communities may be more likely to tap into both local and extra-local resources that can be used to relocate their children to safe spaces. The ability of parents to successfully use exile as a parenting approach for young African American males may significantly reduce the risks associated with living in high-risk impoverished communities.

## The Current Study: Sample and Data

The data used for this chapter were collected from a longitudinal ethnographic study on the social context of adolescent violence among African American youth in New York City. The original research was conducted at the Vera Institute of Justice (1997–2001). The study ethnographically examined the social context of adolescent violence among 15 early adolescent African American males (ages 12–16) and their families living in "Soulville," the pseudonym for a predominately poor, African American subcommunity in Central Harlem.[4] During the study period, Soulville ranked in the top five communities in New York City in homicide, robbery, assault, HIV/AIDS, infant mortality, and tuberculosis. Subjects were recruited for the study in the seventh grade at the Marcus Garvey Junior High School (Garvey), an intermediate school located in Soulville. The study ended when the participants completed ninth grade. An additional year of the study (fourth year) was funded by the Office of Juvenile Justice and Delinquency Prevention to study the emergence of violent youth gangs in Harlem, specifically the Bloods and Crips. Several members of the sample were members of these often-violent youth gangs. The majority of students (98%) at Garvey were eligible for free or reduced school lunch (a key indicator of poverty). Preliminary participant observations of students and discussions were conducted with school staff, including teachers, administrators, counselors, and school security to identify a heterogeneous sample of African American male students. Students were also selected on the basis of academic achievement (honor roll students/students on academic probation); behavior (model students/students in attendance improvement dropout prevention program); involvement in extracurricular activities (i.e., local basketball teams, Boy Scouts, and church choir), and gang affiliation (in this case, the Bloods and Crips). During the first two years of the study (Grades 7 and 8), ethnographic observations were conducted across three contexts: school, the local Soulville community, and the households of each sample member. In the final two years of the study (Grades 9 and 10), ethnographic observations were conducted in the local Soulville community (street corners, recreation centers, parks, arcades, and churches).

Additionally, life-history interviews with both the sample members and their parent(s) were conducted each year of the study. These life-history interviews provide much of the rich and descriptive data for the analysis. Although this study was not specifically intended to examine how poor families devised strategies to keep their children safe, the variety of creative parenting strategies used to save the lives of their sons soon emerged as a theme, particularly the use of exile as a parenting approach for keeping young men safe. During the four-year period of this study, thousands of pages of data were collected, coded, and analyzed using qualitative software (AskSAM).

## Temporary Exile and Permanent Exile

> My brother Tommy comes and spends the night with me on Friday nights because he has a double shift. He drives a bus for Greyhound. On Saturday morning when he leaves Soulville to go back to his home in the Poconos, he'll take my son, Clyde, with him. I love him because he really looks out for my son. I appreciate him helping out because it's really hard being a young Black boy in Soulville. The police are killing all these kids and killing adults too. It's really rough for young Black men out on these streets. (Rhonda Brown, Mother)

For parents in this study, providing adolescents with frequent temporary breaks from Soulville reduced the risks of exposure to local community violence. This strategy is often prompted when parents routinely observe incidents of violent victimization among young Black males in the local community perpetrated by either the police or their peers. Parents such as Rhonda Brown relied on the external familial support of her brother to temporarily take her son Clyde away from Soulville on the weekends. This form of exile, which we have termed temporary exile, does not remove adolescents from the local community and family permanently, but instead provides frequent temporary respites from the local community. Rhonda Brown, a single parent living in public housing in Soulville relied heavily on her older brother Tommy as a valuable form of social capital that she utilized as a community-bridging resource to provide temporary exile for son. For parents with limited financial resources, support provided by other family members to assume childcare duties was perceived as a social responsibility (Jarrett & Burton, 1999). African American uncles played a valuable role in this exile strategy, providing African American male youth with the protective factors necessary for successful adolescent development and positive social/health outcomes (Richardson, 2009).

Rhonda Brown's discussion of temporary exile also provides clear insight into the lack of faith in the police and the criminal justice system experienced by many families living in poor inner-city neighborhoods (Anderson, 1999). During the period of this study, there were several high-profile shootings of unarmed young Black men by the New York City Police Department. None of the victims in these shootings had criminal histories. Consequently, parents and children feared violent victimization in the community by both the gangs and the police, and in some respects among community residents the two groups were synonymous. The field observations and interviews for this study were taking place in the aftermath of the Amadou Diallo shooting, the Abner Louima assault, and the killing of an off-duty security guard by New York City police officers. These three incidents symbolized the climate of police brutality against young Black men in New York City during this period. For parents and children like Rhonda Brown and her son Clyde, exile was a valuable coping mechanism that reduced risk, promoted resilience, and improved safety against violence, including violence perpetrated by the police.

Clyde, the 13-year-old son of Rhonda Brown sums up his vulnerability growing up in Soulville and how temporarily leaving the neighborhood improved his ability to cope with neighborhood violence. He also discusses the valuable role his uncle played in providing him with a safe space and advice on how to cope with neighborhood violence:

> Interviewer: I know at one time, you told me that you wanted to leave Soulville, you called it "Trouble City"?
>
> Clyde: Yeah, I did because it was like everything was going bad, all the violence and stuff, that's why I wanted to leave from here. 'Cause like every time you turn on the news or go outside, you hear about somebody getting stabbed or some girl getting raped or somebody getting shot or beat up by the police.
>
> Interviewer: But how about now? How do feel about Soulville? Do you still feel that way?
>
> Clyde: Yeah a little bit, not a lot, because things are better now, even though there still are a lot of gangs and stuff. I could stay here [Soulville] now because I go to my uncle's house in the Poconos a lot and he talks to me about life and stuff like that so I want to be here now because at least I can get away from here when I want to.

NEW DIRECTIONS FOR CHILD AND ADOLESCENT DEVELOPMENT • DOI: 10.1002/cad

Other parents in the sample used a combination of temporary and permanent forms of exile to save the lives of their sons. In the following narrative, Tina Jackson, a single mother raising two sons, Darnell, 19, and Corey, 13, lived in a small tenement on the southern end of Soulville. Corey's father, Curtis Townsend, had an extensive criminal record and was a high school dropout. He was murdered in Soulville when Corey was 11 years old. Darnell, the oldest son, appeared to be on the same trajectory. At 19 he had been arrested several times for drug possession and was a high school dropout. By the seventh grade Corey seemed to be on a similar path as well. Corey missed more than 35 days of school, putting him at risk of dropping out of school. The school had identified him as a chronic truant, and he was assigned to the school's Attendance Improvement Dropout Prevention Program (AIDP). When I met Tina Jackson, she desperately wanted to move Corey out of Soulville. She feared that he would be dead, incarcerated, or a high school dropout if she did not. She was concerned that as Corey moved through adolescence he would follow the path of his older brother. As Darnell moved further into a life of crime, Corey became the singular focus of Tina Jackson's parenting efforts. In this excerpt, she discusses her problems with her oldest son, Darnell, and the extraordinary efforts she made to keep Corey out of trouble and away from violence in the community:

> Interviewer: As Corey gets older do you have any serious concerns about him?
>
> Tina Jackson: Definitely, especially about being with the right people and going in the right direction. His brother, Darnell, is getting into a lot of trouble being with the wrong crowd. He's 19 and I'm about to kick him out the house because he's not doing anything with his life but hanging with the wrong people, you know, the "do nothing crowd." So you can understand by seeing that, I don't want Corey with the wrong crowd and especially not to hang out on the corners around here. All of my family is so spread out, so we are basically down here alone, and it's rough down here.

Like Rhonda Brown, Tina Jackson was also fearful of the police harassing her son, falsely arresting him, or possibly killing him. Indeed, being violently victimized by the police was perceived as a more life threatening reality than being victimized by a gang. Tina Jackson was another single mother who had a profound distrust of the police and feared that her sons would be violently victimized by the police:

> Tina Jackson: The ghetto is a rough place for a young Black man, there are a lot of policemen doing dirty things to young Black boys around here, they're just looking for young boys to harass, beat up, and lock up. Last week, Darnell was arrested for a mistaken identity for an armed robbery, and had to go to jail for a week. That was the most terrible and miserable thing I've ever been

through. I don't want that to happen to either one of my boys again. That's why I will always send Corey to some type of after school activity outside of this neighborhood, something to keep his mind busy because it's rough out here.

Although Corey resided in a poor, resource-deprived neighborhood, his mother was highly integrated into the local neighborhood's informal social networks, which provided the opportunity to access and command more social capital for Corey's social benefit (Furstenberg, 1999). She was an adept manager at accessing and using these few forms of social capital, such as her church and tenant/block association. She was also quite experienced and knowledgeable in working the system for resources. She placed Corey in her church's summer camp every year. She also registered Corey for the Fresh Air Fund, a program that provided inner-city youth with the opportunity to live in a rural setting with a family for one month during the summer. Each summer Corey lived with the Walden family on a horse farm in Vermont. While in Vermont, he learned how to train and ride horses. The Fresh Air Fund served as another form of community bridging and temporary exile. Tina Jackson and Corey had also forged a close relationship with the Walden family, thus developing additional social capital within their familial network. The following field observations shed light on Tina Jackson's multiple uses of exile:

> When Corey returned to Soulville from Vermont after the completion of the Fresh Air Fund summer program, Tina Jackson enrolled him in a day camp at St. Michael's, a Methodist church located in an affluent community several miles away from Soulville, where he would spend the remainder of his summer engaged in activities supervised and monitored by adults. Over the course of the school year, he attended St. Michael's on the weekends as a member of an arts and crafts group, which allowed him to develop more cultural and social capital.

In the following excerpt, Tina discusses how she located the necessary community-based capital that would open many opportunities for Corey to escape the poverty and violence in Soulville. These community-bridging strategies connected children and their parents with cultural and social capital outside of the local community:

> Tina Jackson: I used to be involved in a lot of things in his afterschool program at his elementary school, and the school provided camping information for kids, they had two camping programs that they were promoting....So I registered him for both camps. He would go to the Fresh Air Fund for a month in July and then St. Michael's for one month in August. I liked the Fresh Air Fund a little more than the other one because I like to keep him out of the city and especially out of Soulville. During the summer months I keep him

in something all the time because I like to keep him off the block and away from the kids in this neighborhood. I make it so he doesn't have to deal with the kids around here [Soulville] day in and day out. This way he has a variety of people, places, and things to see. See the kids around here don't have anything to do, and they get into trouble meddling around in stuff because on this block there are no activities for kids. So I send him away from here to keep him away from all the riff-raff. I feel more comfortable and relieved knowing he's doing something positive and that he's not around here doing nothing but getting into all kinds of trouble.

Corey was also cognizant of the effect that leaving the neighborhood had on his behavior:

Interviewer: So how do you feel about going to all these fun and exciting places?

Corey: I like leaving from around here because my neighborhood is boring. It's dull and dead around here. There's nothing to do around here unless we make up something to do like chase kids and beat them up or something like that.

Fortunately, Tina Jackson also had a wealth of social support within her family. Corey's paternal grandmother, Eldoise Townsend, lived in the northern end of Soulville. She was Corey's surrogate mother and frequently watched him on the weekends. Tina Jackson also used a large network of relatives and friends to monitor Corey's activities. Here she discusses how she maintained and sustained her connections with her extended family members:

Tina Jackson: We do a lot of traveling as a family especially on the weekends. We'll go to a family member's house every weekend and if some members of my family live close by, we'll go visit them too. Usually we go to visit my family members that live in other parts of the city.

Tina Jackson also relied on her sister Janice as a community-bridging resource, as she discusses here:

Tina Jackson: My sister, Janice, Corey's aunt, is a Girl Scout supervisor, and she would always take Corey on trips with her and the Girl Scout troop. Corey liked it, but he was mad that there weren't any boys. So Janice decided to create a Boy Scout troop of five boys. Most were little boys close to Corey's age that lived in her neighborhood. ... The five boys went everywhere the Girl Scouts went. They went to Florida, Disneyworld, Great Adventure, Dorney Park, Radio City Music Hall, Lincoln Center, and the Metropolitan Museum of Modern Art. They were constantly going somewhere and doing all kinds of cultural things together.

However, it was Tina's older brother, Melvin Jackson, who was most intimately involved in Corey's life. Melvin, a former resident of Soulville, had relocated to Dallas, Texas, with his wife, Julia. Melvin worked as a mid-level manager for a large corporation and lived in an affluent Black suburb of Dallas. As a former resident of Soulville, Melvin was intimately aware of the risks and obstacles that could potentially block the successful development of young African American men living in Soulville. When Corey graduated from Garvey Junior High, Melvin approached Tina about sending Corey to live with him in Dallas. In this example of exile, an extended family member (an uncle) suggested that permanent exile would be the best strategy to protect Corey and promote the most effective mechanism for resilience. Initially, Tina was apprehensive:

> Tina Jackson: My brother wants to keep Corey down in Texas because he believes that it will be better for him. I'm contemplating letting him go because it's nice down there and it's more of a country environment, and Corey likes it down there. He gets to go fishing and ride bikes and all kinds of stuff he can't do here in Soulville. My brother doesn't want Corey to be in Soulville anymore. I think my brother wants Corey to change his whole lifestyle and live down there. But my brother keeps pushing it and pushing it, calling here every day, asking, "When are you sending Corey down to stay with me?" But as a mother I'm not sure if I want him to go.

Tina Jackson would later change her mind about sending Corey to Texas after Corey briefly visited Melvin over the summer months. When Corey had returned, he was shocked to discover that his best friend Marcus had been arrested and was in jail:

> Corey: I was kind of mad and disappointed with him [Marcus] because we said we would never do stuff that would make us go to jail. So, I stopped hanging out with him. I just left everybody alone. I had to leave all my friends alone because they were getting into too much trouble, and I wanted to make my family proud and graduate from school.

Weeks after this incident, Corey was assigned to Parkside High School for his freshman year. Parkside had a notorious reputation for violence and youth gangs. Corey's assignment to Parkside and his best friend's arrest changed Tina's mind about permanently exiling him to live with his uncle in Dallas. An excerpt from an interview with Tina Jackson highlights her satisfaction with the decision to permanently exile Corey from the community altogether:

New Directions for Child and Adolescent Development • DOI: 10.1002/cad

Tina Jackson: I'm happy that I sent him to Texas. I miss him, but I figure what's good for him is good for me, too. I want the best for him. I think he has a better chance down there to achieve his goals. There's a better school system there, and from what I saw, the teachers put more time into the kids. They seem to care a little bit more. That just seems to be the way of the South you know, people are more caring and sensitive. If he would have stayed here, I really don't know what the situation might have been, but I would have tried as much as possible to keep him out of these streets and from getting hurt or into trouble. But it would have been rough.

Parents like Rhonda Brown and Tina Jackson utilized relatives who lived outside of Soulville as temporary or permanent safe havens to help their sons escape the threat of violent victimization by the police. Here Ali, a former member of a local Soulville gang, the Valley, discusses how he was sent to stay with his aunt in Queens (a nearby borough) after his close friend, Chris, was involved in a shootout with a rival gang, the Bloods. Ali also describes how Chris was sent to live with relatives in North Carolina (permanent exile) because the Bloods intended to kill him as retaliation for the shooting:

Ali: My best friend, Chris, had to be sent down South because of all this [gang violence]. Now, the Bloods got a hit on him. If he comes back up here to Soulville, they're going to try to kill him. He was down with my crew the Valley [local gang]. But now the Bloods have a hit on him.

Interviewer: What did he do?

Ali: I guess they thought he shot one of them.

Interviewer: So why was he sent to the South?

Ali: He was sent to live with his aunt down south in North Carolina because if he would have stayed here they were going to kill him.

Interviewer: But you were with him during the shootout right? Are they looking for you too?

Ali: Yeah, I was with him, but I didn't shoot anybody though. But since we both down with the Valley and he is my man [friend], they got beef with me too. So my mom and stepfather make me go out to Queens on the weekends to stay with my aunt until things cool down.

Interviewer: So how has that been for you?

Ali: It's cool out there [Queens]. You need to leave Soulville sometimes. You need to go somewhere and experience new things.

Here Carl Long, Ali's stepfather, briefly discusses his thoughts about Ali being sent to Queens on the weekends:

Carl Long: I think it's a positive influence that he goes out there [Queens]. In a sense I would say it's almost more positive than being around here because he gets into less trouble out there and everybody [relatives] gets involved with him over there.

Although Ali's parents had the extra-local resources to provide temporary exile from the violence in Soulville on the weekends, he still faced the threat of gang violence upon his return from Queens. Unlike his friend Chris, who possessed the extended familial resources to be permanently exiled from Soulville, Ali continued to face the threat of violence in Soulville. Here temporary exile may not have been an effective approach for reducing the risk of violent exposure and potential harm:

Interviewer: Do you think it might come down to you having to shoot someone?

Ali: If it comes down to that, that's just how it's got to happen. If they [Bloods] shoot at me, when I go home, I'll get my gun and my people from the Valley, but I'm not just going to be an idiot running around and shooting people though.

Interviewer: But you know, Ali, you're still going to get a gun charge if you get caught carrying a gun? You understand that?

Ali: I understand that.

Interviewer: Do you really understand the consequences of that?

Ali: Look! I don't say nothing to them Bloods. When I pass Bloods in the yard [schoolyard] or on the streets, they don't say nothing to me. And we [the Valley] don't say nothing to them.

Ali and his family also created another safe haven for Ali, albeit a temporary one. Ali participated in a church choir after school. The church was owned by his grandfather, and was in the Bronx, about 10 miles from his home. Ali used the church as a safe space and his own temporary form of exile to distance himself from the violence in his community: "I can bide my time there [church] a lot. I'm in church from like 4:30 until like 10:30

or 11:00 p.m. every day. By the time I leave church its dark and nobody is out on the street."

## Institutional Exile: Relying on the Juvenile Justice System

Several parents in this study, such as Sly and Lydia Howard, did not possess the family-based social capital and a network of relatives they could tap into to provide their son, Sly, Jr., with a safe haven from Soulville. The Howard family lived in public housing in a three-bedroom apartment. Ten people lived in the Howard household, which included Sly, Jr., his parents, Sly's brothers and sisters, and his sisters' children. Unlike other families in this chapter who possessed and utilized both immediate/extended family members as community-bridging resources, Sly's parents did not have any family or community members that they could tap into for support, particularly for youth monitoring/supervision. Although the Howard family had lived in Soulville for over 20 years, they were more socially isolated and less integrated into the local community than other families in this study who lived in Soulville for much shorter periods of time. They could not depend on relatives or neighbors to temporarily or permanently remove their sons from the neighborhood. The Howard family was virtually bankrupt in family and community-based social capital. The following is an excerpt from a conversation with Sly, Sr., describing the absence of social support:

> Interviewer: So besides you and your wife, are there any other significant adults such as family members that you can rely on to watch Sly?
>
> Sly Howard, Sr.: Well, I guess we're about it. This is all the family we've got right here. We're the only two people that Sly will listen to. We're the only two people I guess that can reach Sly.

Sly's parents also lacked socially supportive ties with local neighbors who could assist in supervising and monitoring Sly's activities:

> Interviewer: So around here, in your building and in this neighborhood, do you give older residents the right to reprimand Sly if they see him doing something wrong?
>
> Sly Howard, Sr.: No, I could never do that, it wouldn't work!
>
> Interviewer: How about your neighbors?
>
> Sly Howard, Sr.: No! Because with Sly, I know that I can't reprimand him but so much, so it really wouldn't help matters for them to reprimand, it would make it worse.

By Sly's eighth grade year, he was a member of the MiniMob, a violent youth gang in Soulville. He had been arrested several times for crimes ranging from aggravated assault to armed robbery. The juvenile court had placed him on juvenile probation. He was also selling crack cocaine. Several of his friends whom he sold drugs with had been recently murdered. Sly's mother discusses his reputation as a gangbanger, a crack cocaine dealer, and the death of his friend:

> Interviewer: So do you think Sly's trying to make a name [reputation] in the streets?
>
> Lydia Howard: I don't think. I know. He's making a name for himself now in Soulville.
>
> Interviewer: For being a fighter?
>
> Lydia Howard: For a fighter, for the badness, the ruthlessness, he's a gangster now.
>
> Interviewer: What kinds of drugs is Sly selling—marijuana?
>
> Lydia Howard: I think he is selling crack. That's what he told me he was selling. One thing though I never seen nothin'—he never brings nothin' in here or nothin' like that but he told me what he was doing because I used to ask him, you know. But he said, "Nah, nah," and I used to ask him things. I'd say, "Well what you doin' up on the hill [an area notorious for drug sales]?" He'd say, "Well we just went up on the hill, we didn't do anything up there." One time I was going to go up on the hill there to see what he's doing and it's a good thing that I didn't. I could have gotten myself killed. See his friend just got killed, the same friend he used to hang out with—twenty-one years old—he got killed about two weeks ago up on the hill.
>
> Interviewer: Really?
>
> Lydia Howard: Uh huh, and Sly used to hang with him every day.
>
> Interviewer: How did he get killed—someone shot him?
>
> Lydia Howard: Somebody shot him—up on the hill, he was up there sellin' drugs and takin' people drugs from them. And Sly used to be right there with him.

Frustrated with their inability to discipline Sly and the lack of familial and community support to collectively parent Sly, his parents turned to the most accessible resource available to them for assistance, the juvenile justice

New Directions for Child and Adolescent Development • DOI: 10.1002/cad

system. In order to save Sly from becoming a victim to violence on the streets of Soulville, Sly's parents persistently advocated for the juvenile court to incarcerate their son. For Sly's parents, juvenile detention was their only resource that could provide permanent exile. Sly's mother discusses why she advocated for the juvenile court to incarcerate her son:

> Lydia Howard: I ain't trying to do nothing to hurt Sly. I'm trying to help Sly. I don't want Sly going in the street and doing things like he's been doing, robbing, stealing, selling drugs, and gangbanging, that's why I asked the judge and the probation officer to put him away. I begged them, please don't let him come back home. I told the probation officer I didn't want him to come home, I want him sent away from Soulville to somewhere, any place, far away here, because if they don't, soon me and my husband will be making funeral arrangements for him if he stays on these streets any longer.

The court partially fulfilled Lydia Howard's request and remanded Sly to a group home in Queens roughly twenty miles away from Soulville. While in the group home system, Sly joined another violent youth gang, the Bloods. Following his release from the group home he continued to engage in crime and delinquency. His parents continued to advocate for the juvenile court to detain their son with hopes that incarceration would prevent him from being killed in the streets. Sly was later arrested for another armed robbery and sentenced to a juvenile detention facility in upstate New York. Here Lydia Howard discusses Sly's incarceration:

> Lydia Howard: The way Sly was going, I'm glad he got locked back up again because he was back doing what he continued to do all over again, and you know, he wasn't doing too good. So I said to myself, "everything turned out for the best" because the last thing I need is for him to get killed in the streets.

This example is the most extreme form of permanent exile, where parents advocate for detention as a life-saving measure. This strategy clearly shows the extreme measures desperate parents will take to save their sons from being victims of violence particularly when they have few resources at their disposal.

### Taking Boys Out of the Hood: An Effective Parenting Strategy in Inner-City Neighborhoods?

In Soulville, parents work hard to protect their children from becoming victims of the streets (Anderson, 1999). Some parents and relatives in this study spent a significant amount of time creating strategies to keep their sons from becoming victims of early violent death or incarceration, including "exiling" them from the neighborhood. Parents in this study used both permanent and temporary exile strategies. Single parents like Tina Jackson and the parents of Ali's friend, Chris, decided to permanently remove their sons from the neighborhood to improve their life chances. Other parents such as Rhonda Brown and Carl Long used temporary exile strategies for brief periods of time, primarily during the weekends, as a protective mechanism. Temporary removal from the community often provided less protection because young men still faced the threat of violence once they returned to the local community. However, these temporary breaks seemed to provide the necessary time and separation needed to cope with living in a community besieged with violence. Studies have found that urban adolescents living in high-risk communities may be predisposed to symptoms of psychological stress and PTSD (Berton & Stabb, 1996). Forehand et al. (1991) found that as the number of stressors increase, adolescent functioning deteriorates. With few mental health resources available in poor communities, the parenting strategy of removing children from high-risk neighborhoods even temporarily may serve as a coping mechanism for psychological stress and PTSD.

The findings also suggest that parents who are socially integrated into their local communities and who possess strong family support systems often rely on family members to provide safe havens for their children. In this study, single mothers often relied on their biological brothers for support. These uncles provided safe spaces as well as permanent and temporary guardianship for young men who needed to escape the violence and police brutality associated with living in impoverished communities (Richardson, 2009). Within the family networks in this study, mothers and their children perceived these uncles as valuable forms of family-based social capital. Uncles played a significant role in the collective parenting process. In several instances, uncles assumed the role of a social father. Few research studies have discussed the invaluable role uncles play in the successful adolescent development of African American males. This finding may encourage future research on the socially supportive role of men in African American families, particularly the role of uncles and grandfathers as social fathers.

Conversely, parents like Lydia Howard who possessed very little social capital or informal supportive networks advocated for juvenile detention as a permanent form of exile. Her advocacy for detention provided a glimpse of her desperation as a parent with few resources. However, juvenile detention often produced the opposite effect. Detention often pushed young men further into delinquency, gang affiliation, and increased the potential for violent victimization.

In some cases, the South was used as a safe haven and refuge from the urban violence in the North. Tina Jackson (Texas) and Ali's best friend Chris (North Carolina) all relocated to the South to escape violence in Soulville. Although many southern metropolitan areas (i.e., Atlanta, Memphis, Houston, and New Orleans) statistically have higher rates of violent crime than northern metropolitan areas, many northern Blacks still believe the South provides safer spaces and an improved quality of life for their children (Brown, 2007).

NEW DIRECTIONS FOR CHILD AND ADOLESCENT DEVELOPMENT • DOI: 10.1002/cad

The ability of adolescent males in this study to create their own safe spaces is a testament to the role of human agency which must also be acknowledged. Ali used the church as a resource to keep himself temporarily out of the neighborhood and out of harm's way. The church in many respects was the proverbial saving grace for some young men and their families in this study. Researchers should give more attention to how churches in poor African American communities provide safe spaces for at-risk African American male youth (McRoberts, 2005).

## Future Research

Grady & Ewing's (2005) documentary film *Boys of Baraka* provides a compelling story of poor African American parents living in inner-city Baltimore who were willing to send their adolescent sons to a boarding school (The Baraka School) located in Kenya to escape the violence associated with living in impoverished communities in Baltimore City. Although sending young Black men from inner-city Baltimore to Africa may seem extreme, the central premise of taking boys out of the local neighborhood to an environment where they can feel safe to learn and develop echoes what many parents in this study wanted for their sons. Yet, there are thousands of young men in urban America who have few options to relocate to safer spaces. Parents living in places like Soulville struggle with the everyday reality that when their sons leave home, it is possible that they may never return. In the United States, and specifically in poor urban communities, we have not had great success in providing safe spaces where young men can feel free to learn and develop without the threat of gang violence, police brutality, poverty, an inferior education, and limited prospects for employment. Until we find solutions to these problems, parents and the criminal justice system will continue to "take boys out of the hood."

Future research should explore how parents from various ethnic groups within the African/Latino Diaspora, such as immigrant populations from the Caribbean (e.g., Jamaica, Haiti, Trinidad, Barbados, Dominican Republic, and Puerto Rico) and West Africa (e.g., Nigeria, Ghana, and Senegal), use exile as a parenting strategy. These families often send their children back to their native countries to live with relatives to keep them safe and out of trouble. Pedro Mateu-Gelabert documented the social context of adolescence among Dominican youth and families living in *El Dorado,* a predominately poor Dominican community in New York City. His findings revealed similar strategies of sending children back to the Dominican Republic to keep them safe and out of trouble (Mateu-Gelabert & Lune, 2003, 2007). A comparative qualitative study of parenting strategies among various ethnic groups within the African/Latino Diaspora may provide insight into the similarities, differences, and levels of success in using exile as a parenting strategy for young African American and Latino males.

Future research on parenting strategies for African American youth should focus on successful parenting strategies for adolescent boys and girls. Although the discourse on programs, policies, and practices for young African American males has received significant attention (Edelman, Holzer, & Offner, 2006; Johnson, 2010; Mincy, 2006), we cannot lose sight of parenting strategies to foster successful adolescent development for young Black women living in high-risk neighborhoods. The strategies parents create for African American girls can provide insight into the differences in parenting strategies based on gender. Are girls sent to live with relatives to keep them safe? Are parents with limited resources willing to advocate for juvenile detention for a teenage girl? These are research questions yet to be addressed.

## References

Anderson, E. (1999). *Code of the street: Decency, violence, and the moral life of the inner city*. New York, NY: Norton & Company.

Berton, M. W., & Stabb, S. D. (1996). Exposure to violence and post-traumatic stress disorder in urban adolescents. *Adolescence, 31*, 489–498.

Brezina, T., Agnew, R., Cullen, F. T., & Wright, J. P. (2004). The code of the street: A quantitative assessment of Elijah Anderson's subculture of violence thesis and its contribution to youth violence research. *Youth Violence & Juvenile Justice, 2*(4), 303–328.

Brooks-Gunn, J., Duncan, G. J., & Aber, J. L. (Eds.). (1997). *Neighborhood poverty: Context and consequences for children* (Vol. 1). *Policy implications in studying neighborhoods* (Vol. 2). New York, NY: Russell Sage Foundation.

Brown, C. (1965). *Manchild in the promised land*. New York, NY: MacMillan.

Brown, C. (2007, May 1). Top 10 cities for African Americans 2007. *Black Enterprise*. Retrieved from http://www.blackenterprise.com/mag/top-10-cities-for-african -americans-2007/

Caughy, M. O., O'Campo, P. J., & Muntaner, C. (2003). When being alone might be better: Neighborhood poverty, social capital, and child mental health. *Social Science & Medicine, 57*(2), 227–237.

Centers for Disease Control and Prevention (CDC). (2013). Homicide rates among persons aged 10–24 years—United States, 1981–2010. *MMWR, 62*, 545–560.

Coleman, J. S. (1990). *Foundations of social theory*. Cambridge, MA: Harvard University Press.

Cooper, C., Eslinger, D., Nash, D., Al Zawahri, J., & Stolley, P. (2000). Repeat victims of violence: Report of a large concurrent case-control study. *Archives of Surgery, 135*(7), 837–843.

Cooper, C., Eslinger, D., & Stolley, P. (2006). Hospital-based violence intervention programs work. *The Journal of Trauma, Injury, Infection, and Critical Care, 61*(3), 534–540.

Edelman, P., Holzer, H., & Offner, P. (2006). *Reconnecting disadvantaged young men*. Washington, DC: Urban Institute Press.

Forehand, R., Wierson, M., Thomas, A. M., Armistead, L., Kempton, T., & Neighbors, B. (1991). The role of family stressors and parent relationships on adolescent functioning. *Journal of the American Academy of Child Psychiatry, 30*, 316–322.

Furstenberg, F. (1999). Children and family change: Discourse between social scientists and the media. *Contemporary Sociology, 28*(1), 10–17.

Furstenberg, F. (2000). The family in the city. *Urbana, 5*(26), 25–35.

NEW DIRECTIONS FOR CHILD AND ADOLESCENT DEVELOPMENT • DOI: 10.1002/cad

Grady, R. (Director), & Ewing, H. (Director). (2005). *The boys of Baraka* [Documentary]. United States: Loki Films.

Jarrett, R. L. (1995). Growing up poor: The family experiences of socially mobile youth in low income African American neighborhoods. *Journal of Adolescent Research, 10*(1), 111–135.

Jarrett, R. L. (1997). African American family and parenting strategies in impoverished neighborhoods. *Qualitative Sociology, 20*(2), 275–288.

Jarrett, R. L. (1999). Making a way: Successful parenting in high-risk neighborhoods. *The Future of Children: When School is Out, 9*, 45–50.

Jarrett, R. L., & Burton, L. M. (1999). Dynamic dimensions of family structure in low-income African-American families: Emergent themes in qualitative research. *Journal of Comparative Family Studies, 30*(2), 177–187.

Johnson, W. E. (2010). *Social work with African American males: Health, mental health, and social policy.* New York, NY: Oxford University Press.

Lareau, A. (2002). Invisible inequality: Social class and childrearing in Black and White families. *American Sociological Review, 67*(5), 747–776.

Leventhal, T., & Brooks-Gunn, J. (2001). Changing neighborhoods: Understanding how children may be affected in the coming century. *Advances in Life Course Research, 6*, 263–301.

Lynch, M., & Cicchetti, D. (2002). Links between community violence and the family system: Evidence from children's feelings of relatedness and perceptions of parent behavior. *Family Process, 41*(3), 519–532.

Mateu-Gelabert, P., & Lune, H. (2003). School violence: The bidirectional conflict flow between neighborhood and school. *City & Community, 2*(4), 353–369.

Mateu-Gelabert, P., & Lune, H. (2007). Street codes in high school: School as an educational deterrent. *City & Community, 6*(3), 173–191.

McRoberts, O. (2005). *Streets of glory: Church and community in a Black urban neighborhood.* Chicago, IL: University of Chicago Press.

Mincy, R. B. (Ed.). (2006). *Black males left behind.* Washington, DC: Urban Institute Press.

Morenoff, J. D., Sampson, R. J., & Raudenbush, S. W. (2001). Neighborhood inequality, collective efficacy, and the spatial dynamics of urban violence. *Criminology, 39*(3), 517–558.

Prothrow-Stith, D. (1991). *Deadly consequences.* New York, NY: Harper Collins.

Rich, J. A., & Grey, C. M. (2005). Pathways to recurrent trauma among young Black men: Traumatic stress, substance abuse, and the "code of the street." *American Journal of Public Health, 95*(5), 816–824.

Richardson, J. (2009). Men do matter: Ethnographic insights on the socially supportive role of the African-American "uncle" in the lives of inner-city African-American male youth. *Journal of Family Issues, 30*, 1041–1069.

Sampson, R. J., Raudenbush, S. W., & Earls, F. (1997). Neighborhoods and violent crime: A multilevel study of collective efficacy. *Science, 277*, 918–924.

Smokowski, P. R., Reynolds, A. J., & Bezruczko, N. (1999). Resiliency and protective factors in adolescence: An autobiographical perspective from disadvantaged youth. *Journal of School Psychology, 37*(4), 425–448.

Teplin, L. A., McClelland, G. M., Abram, K. M., & Mileusnic, D. (2005). Early violent death among delinquent youth: A prospective longitudinal study. *Pediatrics, 115*(6), 1586–1593.

Voisin, D. R. (2007). The effects of family and community violence exposure among youth: Recommendations for practice and policy. *Journal of Social Work Education, 43*(1), 51–66.

Wright, J. P., Cullen, F. T., & Miller, J. T. (2001). Family social capital and delinquent involvement. *Journal of Criminal Justice, 29*(1), 1–9.

NEW DIRECTIONS FOR CHILD AND ADOLESCENT DEVELOPMENT • DOI: 10.1002/cad

## Notes

1. There is an impressive body of work on youth resilience, disadvantaged youth overcoming adversity, and how families create ways to reduce the impact of risk for youth in impoverished neighborhoods (Furstenberg, 2000; Leventhal & Brooks-Gunn, 2001; Smokowski, Reynolds, & Bezruczko, 1999).

2. Most recently, the intellectual tradition of community-level research has been revitalized by the increasingly popular idea of social capital. Although there are conflicting definitions, social capital is typically conceptualized as embodied in the social ties among persons and positions (Coleman, 1990; Morenoff, Sampson, & Raudenbush, 2001). Neighborhoods with low levels of social capital are less able to realize common values and maintain the informal controls that foster safety. Sampson et al. (1997) linked community social disorganization to the lack of social capital.

3. There is an impressive body of research that highlights how many parents and families living in high-risk neighborhoods bereft of social capital manage to access and acquire social capital resources to foster safety for their children (Furstenberg, 1999; Jarrett, 1997; Lareau, 2002). Wright, Cullen, and Miller (2001) found that children from families with greater social capital were less delinquent and that social capital was associated with more positive outcomes over the life course. In some studies, the findings suggest that families who possess low levels of social capital experience greater social isolation. Caughy, O'Campo, and Muntaner (2003) examined the relationship between community attachment and behavioral problems in preschool children. They found that in poor neighborhoods, children whose parents knew fewer neighbors were more likely to report problems such as depression and anxiety.

4. Pseudonyms are used throughout this chapter to protect the identities of the participants.

*JOSEPH B. RICHARDSON, JR., is an associate professor of African American studies at the University of Maryland. E-mail: jrichar5@umd.edu*

*MISCHELLE VAN BRAKLE is an assistant professor of criminology at Notre Dame of Maryland University. E-mail: mvanbrakle@ndm.edu*

*CHRISTOPHER ST. VIL is a postdoctoral research fellow in the Department of African American Studies at the University of Maryland. E-mail: cstvil@umd.edu*

NEW DIRECTIONS FOR CHILD AND ADOLESCENT DEVELOPMENT • DOI: 10.1002/cad

Jones, N. (2014). "The regular routine": Proactive policing and adolescent development among young, poor Black men. In K. Roy & N. Jones (Eds.), *Pathways to adulthood for disconnected young men in low-income communities. New Directions in Child and Adolescent Development, 143,* 33–54.

3

# "The Regular Routine": Proactive Policing and Adolescent Development Among Young, Poor Black Men

*Nikki Jones*

## Abstract

*Over the last several decades, proactive policing, in which departments use data on reported crimes to determine where local police officers will target their surveillance, has increased police contact with residents in certain neighborhoods. Drawing on field research conducted over a three-year period (2007–2010) among adult and adolescent African American men in a San Francisco neighborhood with a concentrated poor, Black population, I provide an ethnographic account of routine encounters with the police that structure adolescent boys' daily lives in potentially significant ways. I build on Erving Goffman's discussion of "patterns of mortification" to describe how typical encounters unfold in the day-to-day lives of young men and consider the implications of such encounters for healthy adolescent development. © 2014 Wiley Periodicals, Inc.*

NEW DIRECTIONS FOR CHILD AND ADOLESCENT DEVELOPMENT, no. 143, Spring 2014 © 2014 Wiley Periodicals, Inc.
Published online in Wiley Online Library (wileyonlinelibrary.com). • DOI: 10.1002/cad.20053

James is a 26-year-old African American man who grew up in San Francisco's Fillmore neighborhood.[1] He was born as the crack era dawned in the city, and he came of age during some of his neighborhood's most violent periods. Like many poor, Black men under 30, James has lost friends and family members to the violence of the street— "just so many of them," he tells me during a recorded interview.[2] When I ask if, as an adolescent, he felt like he was in danger of lethal violence, James says, "Yeah, you know. Just being from where I'm from, and you know, it's always something going on. Especially where I'm at, everybody knew that we had problems with other people in our neighborhood and it got escalated to a whole other level" that made "everybody [feel] like a target."

In addition to being vulnerable to violence from other young Black men, James recalls feeling like a target of local police surveillance. He and his peers typically perceived the routine police interventions in their neighborhood as harassment. Over time, they "got used to" these interventions in much the same way they acclimated to the violence in their lives: "We always didn't like it [encounters with police], though. We never liked being harassed; I don't think nobody like that. You know you have to admit that you kinda get use to that too. Just gotta find ways to avoid them, you feel me?"

"Did they stop and frisk you?" I ask.

"Yeah, I been stopped a few times. Regular routine. They got to do the whole search because I'm on probation."

As I sat listening to James, I was struck by his use of the phrase "regular routine." Describing his encounters with the police this way reveals his understanding of these interactions as a frequent and disagreeable part of everyday life, rather than as a periodic, but unpredictable interruption in the normal activities of men and boys on the block. We can recast "regular routine" in sociological terms as *a set of patterned interactions that structure the daily lives of young men in the neighborhood.* These interactions reflect the significant changes in police practices that have occurred over the past several decades. In many metropolitan areas, police departments have shifted from relative abdication of duty in poor communities (a common complaint in the past was that when the police were called, they failed to show up) to visible penetration into areas like James's Fillmore neighborhood (see also Goffman, 2009). One consequence of this trend is that poor, urban Black men in the United States now have the highest rates of involuntary police contacts (Brunson & Miller, 2006). In a report to the United States District Court in 2010, sociologist Jeffrey Fagan concluded that the New York City police department's stop-and-frisk activity was concentrated in precincts with high concentrations of Black and Latino residents and that "NYPD stops are significantly more frequent for Black and Hispanic citizens

NEW DIRECTIONS FOR CHILD AND ADOLESCENT DEVELOPMENT • DOI: 10.1002/cad

than for White citizens" (p. 4). He also found that arrests occur in less than 6% of these cases (see also Rosenbaum, 2007, p. 21).

Other research suggests that "focused police interventions," which include "direct patrols, proactive arrests," and other forms of what is typically described as problem-oriented or proactive policing, can effectively reduce crime rates in "hot spot" areas (Braga, 2008). The underlying logic of these approaches is to focus policing resources on those geographic areas where much of the reported crime occurs. In San Francisco, serious violence is concentrated in 2.1% of the city's 49 square miles. The Lower Fillmore, where I conducted fieldwork over a continuous two-and-a-half year period, falls within this 2.1% of geographic space; the neighborhood was identified in a recent report as one of the five hot spot zones for violence in the city (Braga, Onek, & Lawrence, 2008; SFVPIU, 2011). In an effort to combat crime and violence in these areas, San Francisco implemented problem-oriented interventions, along with other targeted law enforcement practices, during the period in which I was conducting field research in James's Fillmore neighborhood (2007–2010).

Proactive policing practices like hot spot policing have produced mixed results: some evaluations report short-term effects on crime reduction (Braga, 2008), but the research is still out on whether or not targeted policing practices prevent crime over the long term (Rosenbaum, 2006, 2007).[3] There are also potential adverse effects of proactive policing practices that are often overlooked during the course of implementation or evaluation, including the effect of targeted policing practices on police–community relations. Recent ethnographic research suggests that aggressive, targeted enforcement may systematically erode trust in the police, especially among minority youth who are the frequent targets of these encounters (Brunson & Miller, 2006; Rosenbaum, 2007): "Hot spots policing, because it has been operationally defined as aggressive enforcement in specific areas, runs the risk of weakening police-community relations" (Rosenbaum, 2006, p. 253; see also Rios, 2011). This risk is especially acute in poor, minority neighborhoods (Bowling, 1999; Brunson & Miller, 2006; Brunson & Weitzer, 2009; Rosenbaum, 2006; Stewart, 2007).

The erosion of trust in the police is consequential for law-abiding behavior. It is now well accepted in criminological circles that trust in the police is paramount for public safety: people who trust the police tend to obey the law (Rosenbaum, 2006; Tyler, 2006). Further, researchers have found that encounters that are perceived as fair and just are likely to strengthen citizens' beliefs in the legitimacy of law enforcement (National Research Council, 2004). Yet, many studies show that police legitimacy is lower among minority groups (National Research Council, 2004) and in settings in which proactive policing practices are focused (Brunson & Weitzer, 2009). Frequent searches and the failure to find evidence that would lead to an arrest exacerbate tension between neighborhood residents and the police and make young men like James believe that they are arbitrary targets of police surveillance.

In settings like the Fillmore neighborhood where I lived as well as conducted my research, many adolescents—and perhaps especially young Black men—have come to view the police as adversaries. These young men tend to perceive law enforcement (and adjunct authority figures) as institutional actors who treat them with little respect and who are, in general, out to get them (Anderson, 1999; Brunson & Miller, 2006). Such beliefs are only strengthened during the kind of interactions that characterize routine police surveillance. James's reference to "the regular routine" highlights what I observed firsthand: young men in the neighborhood adjust to routine interactions with the police by developing a set of situated strategies designed to help them avoid trouble with the range of law enforcement figures they encounter on the street, from gang or narcotics task force officers to housing security staff. These strategies are deployed with varying degrees of success. Targeted surveillance practices push some young men almost entirely underground as they work to evade all contact with law enforcement; other young men sneak in and out of the neighborhood to visit loved ones and peers. Still others maintain their right to occupy public space. Young Black men who are not "on the run," a term used by locals to describe individuals who are actively avoiding contact with law enforcement (Goffman, 2009), often congregate on neighborhood street corners. It is this claim on public space—a claim they are often reluctant to relinquish (Anderson, 1999)— that positions them as frequent targets of police surveillance.

My field research and interviews with young men in this setting reveals that targeted policing practices do more than shape their perceptions of the police in negative ways; targeted policing practices also shape young people's life space—affecting what they do, where, and with whom. This finding holds not only for those with official criminal histories, but also for other young people in the neighborhood. Developmental psychologists highlight the significant relationship between "life space"—a term used by psychologists to describe the environment that surrounds an individual— and healthy adolescent development this way: "How young people spend their waking hours defines the fund of developmental experiences in each culture; they circumscribe what a boy or girl learns, and for better or worse, shape the men and women these children become" (Larson & Richards, 1989, p. 502). If this is true, then for young Black men who live in high-surveillance neighborhoods, law enforcement officers are now key agents of socialization with a level of authority that may surpass that of teachers, pastors, or parents.

Targeted police practices thus potentially have serious institutional, social, and psychological consequences for adolescent boys as they transition into adulthood. Yet, we know very little about these patterns or their effects. Young men's encounters with law enforcement are rarely subject to observation or evaluation by outsiders. Consequently, adolescent boys must

NEW DIRECTIONS FOR CHILD AND ADOLESCENT DEVELOPMENT • DOI: 10.1002/cad

learn to negotiate directly with police officers who may be a decade or more their senior and who have the authority to use lethal violence. To what extent these experiences shape young men's behaviors and beliefs is unclear, since few researchers have systematically examined how popular policing interventions impact adolescent development.

In this chapter, I contribute to this understudied area of how proactive policing practices shape contemporary adolescence by providing an ethnographic account of the routine encounters that occur in public between young men and the police. I draw on data from multiple sources. Some encounters I observed directly; some information I gathered either by listening to stories of encounters as they were shared among neighborhood residents or learned through formal and informal interviews with locals; and some observations are from a collection of third-party video records (Jones & Raymond, 2012) acquired during the course of my field research in the neighborhood. The recordings were originally collected by Raymond Washington, an African American man who lives in the neighborhood and has used a hand-held digital video camera to record encounters between police and residents for several years. Here, I use transcriptions of selected videos from this archive to illustrate key concepts related to routine encounters between young Black men and the police.

My goal in the pages that follow is to offer a new way to think about the impact of routine encounters between police and citizens, especially minority adolescent males. Instead of asking whether or not targeted surveillance strategies are effective from the perspective of law enforcement, I ask how routine encounters with police on neighborhood streets might influence the healthy development of local adolescents, including both those who are directly involved in interactions with police and those who witness these frequent encounters. How might the regular exposure to such practices influence a young person's developing sense of self (Mead, 1934/1967)? How might such regular interventions shape the daily developmental contexts or the life space (Larson & Richards, 1989) of young men like James? I begin below by briefly describing the field research setting and data collection methods.

## Setting and Method

I took up residence in San Francisco's Fillmore neighborhood in July 2007, less than two weeks after seven people were wounded in a series of early morning shootings, and several months before a permanent gang injunction was issued. That injunction, issued by the city attorney working in collaboration with local law enforcement, restricts the behavior of over 40 alleged gang members in the area around three housing complexes that all occupy the same block in the Western Addition (this is the larger city district of which the Lower Fillmore is a part). Over half of the men listed as gang members in the Western Addition injunction were between the ages of 18

NEW DIRECTIONS FOR CHILD AND ADOLESCENT DEVELOPMENT  •  DOI: 10.1002/cad

and 25 when the injunction took effect. Approximately 90% were 30 years old or younger.

I gained entrée into the neighborhood, and into a small network of men who were working to change their lives, after meeting Eric, an African American man now in his thirties, who had spent the bulk of his adolescence working as a drug dealer in the neighborhood. He had once been part of one of the "gangs" named in the injunction, but Eric is now on a mission to make good. He runs Brothers Changing the Hood (BCH), a small nonprofit organization whose volunteers, mostly other men who are trying to change their lives, work to save Black men in the neighborhood from the violence of the street and to free them from the grip of the criminal justice system. My early introduction to Eric led to 18 months of participant observation with his small organization. In 2008, I helped BCH secure a small grant from the city to conduct outreach with young men named on the neighborhood gang injunction. Our work intensified over this period as I watched Eric use his personal networks to gain access to these individuals, their peers, and family members. I followed Eric's work closely over this 18-month period and continued to follow his work after the grant period ended. In addition to taking copious field notes (about 1000 pages of hand-written field notes), I also conducted one-on-one and group interviews with adult and adolescent men in Eric's network, including four young men named in the neighborhood's gang injunction. The findings presented here are drawn from data collected over this time period.

## Living Under the Gaze of Law Enforcement

For most Americans, encounters with law enforcement are infrequent and typically limited to brief exchanges related to traffic violations. Moreover, the participants—the officer and the citizen—usually are strangers to each other and neither is likely to encounter the other in the future. As James makes clear, for young Black men who live in high-surveillance neighborhoods, interactions with the police are far more regular and much more intimate. As a result, the participants are known to each other in a way that is uncommon in low-surveillance settings.

The neighborhood is neither a jail nor a prison. However, when viewed through a sociological lens, similarities between neighborhood-based police–citizen encounters and patterns of interaction that occur in total institutions (e.g., mental wards, prisons, and jails) emerge. In *Asylums*, Erving Goffman (1959) describes a set of interactions that characterize encounters among staff and captives in total institutions as "patterns of mortification." In institutions like jails and prisons, he writes, these patterns of mortification are "a series of abasements, degradations, humiliations, and profanations of self" (Goffman, 1959, p. 14) that encourage "radical shifts" in a person's "moral career, a career composed of the progressive changes that occur in the beliefs that he has concerning himself and significant others" (p. 14). In detention centers, jails, and prisons, these life-altering patterns of interaction are organized around institutional objectives; specifically, interactions are patterned to reinforce a person's subordinate place in the institutional hierarchy. Goffman's insights draw attention to far-ranging effects of the criminal justice system's historically unique penetration into the daily lives of residents in a neighborhood setting. Below, I describe a variety of routine interactions between police and adolescents in such a setting. I later consider the implications of these interactions for healthy adolescent development.

## Routine Interactions Between Police and Young Men

By the time they enter their teens, boys who grow up in neighborhoods like the Fillmore are aware that the gaze of the police is most frequently targeted at them. The following transcription of a video-recorded exchange illustrates how, in this setting, some youth perceive even nonverbal interaction with the police as intrusive and threatening. The clip opens with the camera focused on a police officer leaning against his squad car, which is parked at a street corner that is a popular hangout for neighborhood youth. The voice of a young man calls out to Ray, the cameraman:

"Get 'em Ray. They [the police] was harassing me the whole day. You feel me? Get all that Ray he was harassing me," the young man says.

"This one cat [officer]—right here?" Ray asks.

"Both of 'em," the young man explains.

"Oh it's two in there [the car]?"

"There's another one. They was both harassing me. He right there in the car. Get all of it [on camera]."

"What was they talking about?" Ray asks.

"They talking 'bout we can't stand by the bus stop. First they came searching right there for nothing. Then we can't stand at the bus stop."

"They say you can't stand at the bus stop?"

"Yeah and they just sat here and watched us for a good, what, five, ten minutes?"

"Right."

"They sat right there."

"Watch to see if a bus come or something."

"Uh, huh. Man, they crazy."

"Yeah."

"Wow."

"Y'all got to call me sooner."

After a few moments of being filmed, the officer gets back in his car and drives off.

In areas that adopt proactive policing practices, these types of encounters are routine. Officers are encouraged to spend time in areas where crime or violence is concentrated even if it appears as if nothing is happening. It is impossible for a young man to truly know the officer's intention, yet his framing of the officer's presence and gaze as harassment is illustrative of how even the most minimally intrusive encounters—a look, a stare—can signal to young men that that they are locked in "a forced social relationship" with law enforcement (Goffman, 1959, p. 23). In this case, the young man reports feeling watched while engaging in a routine act like hanging out at a bus stop; his encouragement of Ray to "get" the officer on camera is a form of retaliation. The young man perceived the officer's gaze as a deliberate intrusion upon his life space and he now wants Ray to make the officer experience a similar level of discomfort. Yet the gaze of law enforcement is quite different from the gaze of a citizen. A look or stare from a police officer can coerce a citizen into participating in what sociologist Harold Garfinkel describes as a public degradation ceremony "whereby the public identity of an actor is transformed into something looked on as lower in the local scheme of social types" (Garfinkel, 1956, p. 420). The young man's interpretation of the officer's gaze as "harassment" suggests that he understands the officer's behavior as a message: He is not free to hang out on the block without becoming a subject of law enforcement surveillance. He is, even if not a suspect, always suspect.

Currently, we know little about the developmental consequences of encounters like this one. Goffman (1959), however, argues persuasively that in total institutions, such interactions are intended to injure a person's self. In the military, the objective is to break down the self and then build up a new self in service to the institution: a soldier. In prisons, the objective is to reaffirm the lower status of the incarcerated in order to reinforce the social hierarchy of the institution. But what are the consequences of such encounters for young men in a neighborhood like the Fillmore? In these settings, such encounters, especially if they are regular features of daily life, are likely to injure a young person's sense of self, as such practices do in other institutional settings. In addition, however, because these interactions with law enforcement are likely to occur at a key stage in a young person's developmental trajectory, they may do more than influence what a young man does, with whom, and how. These encounters also may inform a young man's sense of who he is, who he can become, his commitment to mainstream society, and, ultimately, his beliefs in the fairness and legitimacy of policing.

That these sorts of interactions are unwelcome and potentially injurious is revealed in the effort young men put into *avoiding* them. Young people in troubled neighborhoods often develop situated survival strategies that help them successfully navigate their environment (Jones, 2010). The strategies used by adolescents in the Fillmore are similar, but they are distinguished by their specific relationship to the presence of law enforcement. One common defensive strategy is what I refer to as "the walk-around." The goal of this maneuver is to keep its user(s) out of the sightlines of police officers. As the police approach, young men, especially if they are in a group, disperse and walk in the other direction. In some cases, the young men may be fulfilling an informal deal made with local beat officers: they avoid direct interaction with the police and potentially an arrest for involvement in illegal behavior and the police officers avoid investing the time and energy required to process a nonfelony arrest.[4] Avoidance strategies do not always work. In the federally subsidized housing complex nearest my home, young men escaped view by slipping into the gated interior area of the complex. This would offer some respite from the police, but it would frequently place them into the sightlines of housing security personnel, who also were intent on displacing them. In addition, sometimes young men are caught in what feels to them like "surprise attacks" in which police cars pull up quickly and officers aggressively confront an individual or a small group of young people. Boys as young as 12 and 15 shared accounts of police officers "jumping out [of their cars] on us," with their weapons drawn. During a meeting held in the neighborhood, one young man described his experience with a surprise attack. After he shared his story, I asked him how he responded when officers jumped out on him with weapons drawn. The teenager leaned back in his chair, extended his arms outward, and raised his palms in the air: "I don't do nothing," he said with a resigned shrug.

## "Going in My Pockets": The Intimate Dance of the Stop-and-Search

In a setting that embraces proactive policing practices, body searches are common. "Going in my pockets" is a colloquial term youths use to describe these routine searches. The walk-around is aimed at avoiding this type of encounter. Routine searches can lead to an arrest, but often they do not (Fagan, 2010). In some jurisdictions, law enforcement may record such encounters as a "stop-and-frisk" or a "pat down." Legal scholars typically describe these encounters as "Terry stops," a reference to the 1968 precedent-setting Supreme Court decision in *Terry v. Ohio*. The Fourth Amendment protects the rights of citizens from unreasonable searches and seizures. Reaching into a person's pockets or patting down their clothing constitutes a search. Whenever a police officer stops an individual and restrains his freedom to walk away, that person is effectively "seized." Prior to *Terry v. Ohio*, the Supreme Court held that police officers must have probable cause to initiate such encounters. In *Terry v. Ohio*, the justices ruled that the initiation of such interactions could meet a lesser standard, namely, "whether a man of reasonable caution is warranted in believing that the action taken was appropriate" (*Terry v. Ohio*, 1968, "Syllabus," 5[b]). This standard is commonly referred to as "reasonable suspicion." In some settings, the stop-and-search is now used with a regularity that defies reason (Fagan, 2010; Fagan, Geller, Davies, & West, 2009). For young Black men in these settings, the stop-and-search has become a regular routine.

The stories young men shared in public meetings and in formal and informal conversations reveal common characteristics in the unfolding of a "going in my pockets" kind of encounter. These searches usually begin with an officer approaching an individual or a small group of young men who are hanging out on the block. Once within arm's distance or so, the officer asks the young man for identification.[5] If he has it, the young man shows his identification. The officer may review the identification, call into the station for verification, or check it against lists accessible from his squad car. Alternatively, the officer may simply glance at the ID to check the address shown against the address where the young man has been stopped. Over the last decade, federally subsidized housing complexes have increased the enforcement of trespassing laws in and around their properties. Violations of these laws can be grounds for citation or arrest (Beckett & Herbert, 2010).

During the search, the officer might refer to the target in informal ways, such as "dog" or "G"; doing so signals the officer's sovereign power to "automatically assume the right to employ an intimate form of address or truncated formal ones" (Goffman, 1959, p. 31). If the young man protests or complains during an encounter, the officer may choose to address some concerns, but not others, or may simply ignore complaints and conduct the search largely in silence. If the ID is valid and the search continues without escalation to arrest, then the officer will release the young man.[6]

In other cases, the officer might not request identification and may simply direct a young man to hold his arms up in the air or place his hands against a nearby wall. The officer may then pat down the individual's outer clothing. The young man may participate in the search in an effort to bring the encounter to an end more quickly. An officer who intends to place his hands deep inside a young man's pockets may first ask if the person has anything (e.g., a weapon or anything sharp) in his pockets. Otherwise, he might just squeeze the outside of the pockets first. If the officer finds no illegal substances, he may ask the young person a series of questions, seeking information about other people or other cases, or he may just let him go.[7]

**Behaving Like a Professional Suspect.** A stop-and-search encounter demands either explicitly or implicitly that a young man accept a "submissive or supplicant" role, since serious challenges—intended or perceived—to an officer's authority can lead to a loss of liberty or, in extreme cases, loss of life. By the time they are in their late teens, young men who are frequent targets of the police have learned how to behave as professional suspects. In some cases, the stop-and-search can be accomplished with little more than nonverbal communication. The search I describe below was captured on video and is part of the video archive of interactions between police and Fillmore residents. The clip illustrates how young men have been socialized into participating in these encounters.

The clip begins with two people in the frame—a White male officer dressed in plain clothes and a young Black man wearing a black hoodie. (In this neighborhood, the black hoodie is a standard part of the urban youth uniform.) The officer's blue striped polo shirt makes him stand out as an outsider. The officer has the build of an outside linebacker and is about a foot taller than the young man. The two stand chest-to-chest. The young man, who appears to be in his late teens, looks directly at the officer, but the officer's gaze is directed at the young man's left pocket. The officer's right hand grips the young man's outstretched right arm. The teen's other arm is lifted slightly above a 90° angle:

> "What?" says the young man, as he drops his arm to his side, "What the fuck you talking about?"

The officer keeps his hold on the teen's right arm and begins lifting the hoodie. The young man grabs his sweatshirt and lifts it himself, exposing his belly and part of his lower chest. The two look toward the young man's right pants pocket. The officer moves his left hand to the teen's jeans, which hang slightly below his hip, exposing an inch or two of his boxer shorts. The teen holds his sweatshirt up near his midchest line. The officer holds his right hand in the air as he moves his own left hand across the young man's pockets:

> "Did I talk about anything?" the officer asks, in response to the question the teen posed a couple of seconds earlier.

The officer glances at the camera and continues the search. The teen is still using both hands to hold his sweatshirt up. The officer places his right hand on the teen's upper right arm, and the teen turns around. The two are now standing back to chest. The officer's back is to the camera. The officer reaches his hand down the right leg of the teen:

NEW DIRECTIONS FOR CHILD AND ADOLESCENT DEVELOPMENT • DOI: 10.1002/cad

"I ain't got nu'n' sharp, nigga. I don't carry weapons, nigga," says the teen as he is turned around.

The two begin to turn to their left. The young man's sweatshirt starts to drop back down toward his waist. His pants have slipped, so that his studded black belt now hangs below his buttocks. The officer places his left hand on the teen's left arm:

"Don't use that word. It's a bad word," the officer says to the teen.

For a moment, the officer turns chest-to-chest toward the teen. As he does, the teen lifts both arms directly above his head. The officer offers a quick, dismissive glance and then turns and walks quickly away from the teen:

"That's just my slang," the young man says, and begins to follow the officer, who is walking toward his partner (who is searching a peer of the teen the camera was focused on).

"It's still a bad word," says the officer over his shoulder.

"Man, right," says the youth.

The portion of the search described above lasts less than 15 seconds, but the interactions embody the routine and reveal its accompanying patterns of degradation. As the officer moves silently through each step of the search, the teen moves along with him, following the officer's nonverbal direction at each turn. The officer does not tell the youth to keep his arms raised, but he does; he does not tell the young man to hold up his sweatshirt, but he does so, seemingly anticipating the officer's next move. The officer does not tell the youth to turn around, but he follows the pull of the officer's arm, as if the two are in an intimate dance. The teen also seems aware that the officer is looking for weapons. He anticipates a body search: "I ain't got nu'n' sharp, nigga. I don't carry weapons, nigga." Carefully reviewing this recorded encounter makes clear that the stop-and-search is "a set of structured social routines understood and enacted by the various parties involved" (M. Sullivan, personal communication). In short, it is a "regular routine."

In addition to the nonverbal messages about how to play his role in the stop-and-search, the teen at each turn also receives messages about his relative inferiority vis-à-vis the police: He is, sometimes physically, constrained in a submissive role. He may offer some verbal challenges, but officers have a great deal of discretion in choosing a response. The officer in the clip does not address the substance of the teen's complaints. Instead, he responds in the most literal sense ("Did I talk about anything?") and adds an admonishment against using a "bad word." Alternatives to dismissing the complaints of targets of stop-and-search encounters include teasing the targets, denying their complaints, or deliberately lengthening encounters with repeated questioning. In these situations, the targeted individuals find themselves enmeshed in a "developing tissue of constraint" (Goffman, 1959, p. 41). They are released from these constraints only at the direction and authority of the officer—who may demonstrate that authority with no more than a quick final glance before walking away from the targeted individual.

**Catch and Release.** In total institutions, routine searches like the one described above communicate dispossession (Goffman, 1959). In the neighborhood, these routine searches send the message that a Black, young, male body is state property. This is perhaps most evident in strip searches. In such cases, which I describe as "catch and release," the search on the street leads to detention or arrest, and to a subsequent, and far more invasive strip search at the local police station. The strip search is not always followed with long-term detention, which gives this process a "catch-and-release" feel. This procedure is especially demeaning because it leaves the reason for the humiliating search unresolved. It is emasculating as a practice, but the humiliation is magnified as young men may see officers who have seen the most intimate parts of their bodies patrolling the neighborhood after they are released.

## Police Interactions, Adolescent Development, and Secondary Trauma

The stop-and-search is a meaningful encounter for the young people directly involved. Likewise, the vicarious experience of witnessing such encounters significantly affects young onlookers (Brunson, 2007). Beyond reaffirming negative attitudes toward the police, witnessing exposes neighborhood residents to a secondary shame and degradation. Adolescents may be especially vulnerable. Typically, bystanders are aware that there is little they can do to stop an unfolding police encounter. This powerlessness results in an experiential mortification: "an individual witnesses a physical assault upon someone to whom he has ties and suffers the permanent mortification of having (and being known to have) taken no action" (Goffman, 1959, pp. 33, 35). Repeated experiences are likely to erode witnesses' trust in the police.

An example of young bystanders' sense of powerlessness emerged during a weekly meeting for adolescent boys that I attended. The meetings are regularly led by Lincoln, an African American man and former drug dealer who acts as a social father to several local youth, helping them and their peers process difficult events in the neighborhood, including the social meaning of arrests. As the description below (based on a field note I wrote shortly after the meeting) indicates, I both observed and participated in this meeting.

I arrive at one of the meetings and a group of about 12 boys is arranged around the tables, which are shaped like an L. When Lincoln asks if I have anything to say to the boys, I say I do not. Lincoln does. He asks the group what they think about Ed getting beat up. When I ask who Ed is, Lincoln tells me he is the son of the housing complex's maintenance worker, and that it was the police who beat him. He explains that the police got a call that a Black man wearing a white T-shirt had a gun. That description (as Lincoln notes) is broad enough to fit everyone present. When the police arrived, they arrested Ed, handcuffed him, and then slammed him to the ground. Lincoln says he has never seen that (slamming a cuffed suspect to the ground) happen before. Ed had a cut on his head, above his eyebrow, and he resisted getting thrown into the back of the police car. Once forced inside, he kicked out the back window.

Some of the boys at the meeting witnessed this dramatic scene; they seem saddened and frustrated by the events. I ask the whole group how that kind of an event makes them feel. One boy says that it makes you feel like you want to hurt the police. When I say that I can understand that feeling, Lincoln counters quickly, reminding the boys that they cannot hurt the police. He then returns to my original question, asking about their feelings. One of the younger boys, about 12 years old, answers, saying that what happened to Ed makes him feel like it is racist, like the police do not like Black people, like they deliberately go after the older Black men, so that just young boys like them are going to be left, and then they will need a pass to get on housing complex property.

I ask if the treatment of Ed makes them feel like the police are there for them. They say no, adding that the police do not care if somebody gets shot. When I question how it makes them feel about power, one boy says he feels like he has no power. I probe, repeating his answer, which he confirms. Then I ask the group what they can do if they have no power. Stay out of trouble, do well in school, one boy suggests. Pressing, I ask, what else? The often boisterous group falls silent.

The sort of paralysis and powerlessness revealed in these young men's remarks is a consequence of what Goffman describes as experiential mortification. They know there is little they can do, either to stop the police from injuring someone they care for and respect or to shield themselves from similar demonstrations of power. They conclude that the police "don't like" Black people (see also Brunson, 2007), and they envision a time when they too will be targeted for removal from the neighborhood. When asked what they can do to avoid this sort of experience, they focus primarily on strategies for staying out of trouble and then fall silent, suggesting that they can think of no other effective response to what they see as arbitrary and discriminatory demonstrations of power and force by the police.

## "Paperwork" and the Policing of Peer and Family Networks

On the street, young Black men are open to both voluntary and involuntary contact with the police. Those on "paperwork" (a term used by young men, and sometimes by officers, to refer to a person's set of official ties—such as parole or probation—to the juvenile or criminal justice system) are especially vulnerable. Probationers and parolees are required to essentially waive their Fourth Amendment protections as a condition of their release. In San Francisco, release conditions include consent to a search of home or person performed by a California Peace Officer at any time of day or night. In addition to parole and probation orders, other sorts of paperwork, like the Western Addition gang injunction, also increase neighborhood residents' vulnerability to encounters with police. By definition, a gang injunction restricts the behavior of those named on the injunction, when these people are in a specific geographic area or areas (the injunction zone(s)). Otherwise legal behavior, like associating with others named on the list, is a violation if it occurs within the injunction zone. Policing a gang injunction thus encourages preemptive surveillance: once an injunction is in place, police officers are often encouraged to patrol the area looking for people who are in violation.

Interviews Eric and I conducted with young men in the neighborhood indicate that the policing of gang injunctions increases the intensity of surveillance and, in turn, reorders relationships with family and friends. A common refrain among young men living in the gang injunction zones is that the aggressive policing—which involves housing security staff, uniformed officers, and gang task force members—disrupts their family and extended family networks.[8] Tré, a 21-year-old, African American man who participated in a group interview with Eric and me, describes what it feels like to live in the gang injunction safety zone:

> I feel like the gang injunction, it's a way of separating people... like people who I might have grown up with all my life. I might have grown up with them and then now they come with this gang injunction ... they should have [called] it, it should be [called a] family injunction. I mean like people I grew up with, I'm twenty-one right now and people I been playin' in the sandbox since I was five with, you know, they tryin' to tell them you're a gang, you can't be with him. You know? And it be somebody that's like family, like my cousin or one of my brothers or somethin' that I grew up with all my life, and [now] they separating us.

Ironically, Tré is *not* listed on the gang injunction. Nevertheless, he feels as though he is: "Yeah, it go both ways. I'm not on the gang injunction personally, but I feel like I'm on the gang injunction, my family and my friends are on the gang injunction. So it feels like I am on the gang injunction." The policing of the gang injunction, in a setting that is already under heavy

New Directions for Child and Adolescent Development • DOI: 10.1002/cad

surveillance, prompts this young man to change whom he interacts with, where, and in what ways.

Tré's account draws attention to how the penetration of the criminal justice system into the neighborhood alters the standard trajectory for healthy transitions into adulthood. His world is getting smaller during a life stage when it should be expanding. As children, he says, he and his peers played in the sandbox under minimal surveillance. As they are transitioning into adulthood, Tré and his "street family" are experiencing a tightening of surveillance that severely limits their patterns of behavior and association.

Another 21-year-old man, who is a father and lives in a different part of the neighborhood that is also under a gang injunction, holds a belief similar to Tré's regarding the targeting of family and peer networks and the enforcement of gang injunctions:

> I used to spend the night, we used to really, like, spend the night at each other houses, we used to go to school together. You know, go to after-school programs all this, going on field trips with your summer programs and, you know, [we] grew up together, like, really grew up together. Like, it was [we were] with each other every day and now that we done moved back in these apartments, we reunited, and they're tryin' to call us a gang.

In both this young man's remarks and in Tré's we see the gradual criminalization and increased surveillance of their family, peer, and street family networks. They move from the sandbox, to after-school programs, to being officially identified as gangs. As they enter their early twenties they have, or feel as if they have, an official criminal status.

Both young men's comments also suggest that a different, more natural trajectory has been interrupted or aborted. As members of an adolescent peer group, these young men could be expected to move from spending the night at each other's homes, to taking excursions on field trips, to moving independently into the broader world. Instead, the official label of "gang member," combined with targeted police practices already in place, restricts their mobility and freedom of association, effectively shrinking their social worlds until they feel, as my key respondent once put it, "locked on the block." In other, more stable settings, as youth transition into adulthood, their social worlds expand. They may go off to college or to full-time jobs, where they experience freedoms that encourage further growth and development.

The experiences of young men like the ones I describe in this chapter are more typically viewed through the lens of criminal justice or public safety. In many places where local, state, and federal law enforcement agencies have embraced targeted policing practices, drops in crime are used as evidence that such strategies work. But what would the evidence suggest if we also measured the impact of targeted policing practices on healthy adolescent development? In the next section, I consider this question and suggest new directions for future research.

## Proactive Policing and Positive Adolescent Development

Adolescence is generally seen as a time "when individuals begin to explore and examine psychological characteristics of the self in order to discover who they really are, and how they fit in the social world in which they live" (Steinberg & Morris, 2001, p. 91). In general, increased psychological autonomy and a widening of one's life space mark this developmental period (Steinberg & Morris, 2001). The findings presented here suggest that routine exposure to proactive policing practices holds the potential to influence more than the life space of poor, minority youth. To return to Goffman's analysis for a moment, total institutions like jails and prisons are characterized by an echelon-based system of authority meaning that "any member of the staff class has certain rights to discipline any member of the inmate class, thereby markedly increasing the probability of sanction" (Goffman, 1959, p. 42). As Goffman explains, "the only echelon authority [most persons] must face—the police—is typically not constantly or relevantly present." For poor, young Black men who live in high-surveillance neighborhoods, however, the police typically *are* "relevantly present," and encounters with their echelon authority are a routine feature of these adolescents' lives. Youth are also interacting with these authoritarian figures at time when they are psychosocially immature and the cognitive functioning they need to make mature decisions is still developing (Steinberg & Scott, 2003). Research on the experiences of adolescents at the earliest stages of involvement with the criminal justice system—entry—reveals that adolescents are generally not capable of understanding the implications of their interactions with the justice officials. In general, adolescents' "basic cognitive and reasoning abilities are less mature than those of adults" (Grisso & Schwartz, 2000, p. 2). Youth are also "likely to be less knowledgeable than adults about the legal process" (Grisso & Schwartz, 2000, p. 2). For example, researchers have found that younger adolescents demonstrate a poor understanding of all four of the Miranda Rights (Grisso & Schwartz, 2000).

In settings where targeted policing practices have proliferated, it is increasingly difficult to completely avoid voluntary or involuntary contact with the police (Fagan, 2010). Research on parenting, authority, and positive social development encourages us to think more deeply about how routine encounters with law enforcement might influence, and potentially interrupt, normative adolescent development. For example, research on the influence of parenting styles on adolescent development has found that authoritarian parenting styles—a style of parenting that is high in demandingness but low in responsiveness, does not encourage healthy adolescent development. In contrast, an authoritative style of parenting that is high

NEW DIRECTIONS FOR CHILD AND ADOLESCENT DEVELOPMENT • DOI: 10.1002/cad

in demandingness *and* high in responsiveness leads to more positive outcomes among youth (Steinberg, Mounts, Lamborns, & Dornbusch, 1991). Policing is inherently an authoritarian enterprise. Any police–citizen interaction demands some minimal measure of compliance on the part of the civilian. Typically, compliance is given voluntarily; if it is not then police officers may use a range of force options to gain the compliance that is demanded of an encounter. In short, a civilian must be responsive to an officer, but it is not required that an officer be responsive to a civilian. We do not yet know if the same sort of relationship between authoritarian parenting and adolescent development holds true for authoritarian policing and adolescent development, but we do know that some law enforcement interventions have negative impacts on normative adolescent trajectories. For example, researchers have found that being arrested as a juvenile leads to increased chances of dropping out of high school, which increases probability of unemployment and future involvement in criminality (Rosenbaum, 2007). Future research should continue to explore how involvement with the criminal justice system at the earliest stages of adolescent development may influence or interrupt positive adolescent development.

## Discussion

When crime reduction is the highest priority, the most pressing question is, do targeted policing practices decrease rates of crime, violence, or victimization? Recent research reveals that even in very troubled settings, most of the violent crime is committed by a small number of people, but with respect to people (as opposed to physical space), targeted policing practices cast a much wider net. As a result, even young men who are not officially labeled as criminals may feel criminalized.

Policymakers, practitioners, and scholars would do well to use a broader lens than public safety alone when evaluating the effects of targeted policing practices. I conclude this chapter by offering four questions that should be considered in conjunction with public safety concerns:

1. *What are the consequences of proactive policing practices for healthy adolescent development?* In *Asylums*, Erving Goffman writes that each encounter with an institutional authority is a sort of "trimming procedure," consisting of efforts to draw captives into the "administrative machinery of the establishment... to be worked on smoothly by routine operations" (Goffman, 1959, p. 16). Officially, young neighborhood men are not "captives," but their descriptions of the stop-and-search as routine indicate that they are the subjects of a trimming procedure. Does this routine trimming encourage them to move freely in the world, as other youth are encouraged to do at this stage in their development? Or, do these practices encourage young men to pull back from mainstream society and the obligations and responsibilities that usually accompany early adulthood?

2. *How do targeted policing practices influence the development of pro-social peer networks during adolescence?* Targeted policing practices, which are often responses to calls from within the community and city hall to "do something" about crime and violence in the neighborhood, can criminalize—either officially or by association—adolescent peer networks at key developmental stages. Researchers from a range of disciplines agree that delinquency and deviance are normal features of adolescent development (Farrington, 1995; Steinberg & Morris, 2001). In low-surveillance settings, it is possible that youth are likely to experiment with delinquency and deviance with less surveillance from law enforcement. Since they experience less surveillance than youth in neighborhoods that adopt targeted policing practices, they are also less likely to receive an official criminal sanction for their behavior. Without any official intervention, it is quite likely that these youth will drift in *and out* of delinquency.[9] How might proactive policing influence this trend? It is possible that targeted policing practices might make it more difficult for young people to drift out of delinquency. Punishing youth for relatively low-level infractions may increase their attachment to peers who are more deeply involved in serious delinquency. In addition to increasing the likelihood of receiving an official criminal sanction, targeted policing practices may unintentionally encourage the development of a new generation of delinquent youth in high-surveillance settings. Future research should explore the extent to which the penetration of police practices into young men's peer and family networks gives neighborhood youth a criminalized identity, and keeps them linked to the juvenile or criminal justice system and to peers who are more deeply committed to delinquency or criminal behavior.

3. *How do targeted policing practices influence adolescents' understanding of healthy masculinities?* On the block, targeted policing practices often encourage adolescent boys to act like grown men, while possessing only the skills and knowledge developed in and through their interactions with law enforcement. These encounters teach teenaged boys that manhood is about dominance, control, and authority. This understanding does not necessarily encourage healthy masculinity, especially among young men whose experiences with the police often leave them feeling powerless. Targeted policing practices can encourage young men to prove their manhood through aggression, directed against others, including male and female peers and intimates. Policing practices also can encourage young men to act like children, as they sneak away from the gaze of authority at a period in their lives when they should be transitioning into healthy adulthood.

4. *How do routine encounters with the police influence a young person's developing sense of self?* Much of the research on police–citizen encounters is concerned with the use of force, especially police brutality (see

Terrill, 2003, for a review of this research). Recent research encourages a shift to examining how frequent targets of police–citizen encounters interpret their experience and the implications of these interpretations for trust in the police more generally (Brunson & Miller, 2006). My data and analysis bring a related concern to the forefront: how do *routine* encounters with the police impact a young person's developing sense of self? Routine encounters typically involve young men interacting directly with institutional authority at an age when they lack the full capacity to do so. Just as importantly, these encounters with police authority send messages, both to the young men directly involved and to bystanders, about their place in mainstream society. Whether target or witness, the message received is the same: although not quite a prisoner, a poor, young Black man does not have command over his own world. He is a contradiction: free, but not free. Future research should explore the range of negative emotions—including terror, anxiety, shame, and anger—that are engendered by living this contradiction, and investigate the consequences of these life experiences for a young person's developing sense of self.

The policing practices I have described are likely to alter key developmental processes in ways that are not yet fully appreciated. Findings from my field research suggest that our current conversation about targeted policing practices is too narrowly focused. Public safety is important, but so is healthy adolescent development. To this end, future research should focus on the range of developmental consequences that emerge as a result of routine encounters between young men and the police.

### References

Anderson, E. (1999). *The code of the street: Decency, violence and the moral life of the inner city*. New York, NY: Norton Press.

Beckett, K., & Herbert, S. (2010). *Banished: The new social control in urban America*. New York, NY: Oxford University Press.

Bowling, B. (1999). The rise and fall of New York murder: Zero tolerance or crack's decline? *British Journal of Criminology, 39*, 531–554.

Braga, A. A. (2008). *Crime prevention research review No. 2: Police enforcement strategies to prevent crime in hot spot areas*. Washington, DC: U.S. Department of Justice Office of Community Oriented Policing Services.

Braga, A., Onek, D., & Lawrence, S. (2008, November). *Homicide and serious gun violence in San Francisco*. Presentation prepared for the Berkeley Center for Criminal Justice. Retrieved from http://bit.ly/1akbRff

Brunson, R. (2007). "Police don't like Black people": African American young men's accumulated police experiences. *Criminology & Public Policy, 6*, 71–102.

Brunson, R. K., & Miller, J. (2006). Young Black men and urban policing in the United States. *British Journal of Criminology, 46*, 613–640.

Brunson, R. K., & Weitzer, R. (2009). Police relations with Black and White youths in different urban neighborhoods. *Urban Affairs Review, 44*, 858–885.

Fagan, J. (2010, October). Report of Jeffrey Fagan, Ph.D., to United States District Court, Southern District of New York. David Floyd et al. (plaintiffs), against,

City of New York et al. (defendants). Retrieved from http://ccrjustice.org/files/Expert_Report_JeffreyFagan.pdf

Fagan, J., Geller, A., Davies, G., & West, V. (2009). Street stops and broken windows revisited: The demography and logic of proactive policing in a safe and changing city. In S. K. Rice & M. D. White (Eds.), *Race, ethnicity, and policing: New and essential readings.* New York: New York University Press. Retrieved from http://ssrn.com/abstract=1399073

Farrington, D. (1995). The development of offending and antisocial behavior from childhood: Key findings from the Cambridge study in delinquent youth. *Journal of Child Psychology and Psychiatry, 36,* 1–35.

Garfinkel, H. (1956). Conditions of successful degradation ceremonies. *American Journal of Sociology, 61*(5), 420–424.

Goffman, A. (2009). On the run: Wanted men in a Philadelphia ghetto. *American Sociological Review, 74,* 339–357.

Goffman, E. (1959). *Asylums: essays on the social situation of mental patients and other inmates.* New York, NY: Anchor Books.

Gordon, R. (2005, August 5). Western Addition deadliest city area. 3rd slaying in 8 days prompts response from police, mayor. *San Francisco Chronicle.* Retrieved from http://www.sfgate.com/bayarea/article/SAN-FRANCISCO-Western-Addition-deadliest-city-2618419.php

Grisso, T., & Schwartz, R. G. (2000). *MacArthur Foundation Research Network on adolescent development and juvenile justice. Executive Summary.* Retrieved from http://www.adjj.org/downloads/5986Youth%20on%20Trial.pdf.

Hiibel v. Sixth Judicial District Court of Nevada, 542 U.S. 177 (2004).

Jones, N. (2010). *Between good and ghetto: African American girls and inner-city violence.* New Brunswick, NJ: Rutgers University Press.

Jones, N., & Raymond, G. (2012). "The camera rolls": Using third-party video in field research. *ANNALS of the American Academy of Political and Social Science, 642,* 109–123.

Larson, R., & Richards, M. (1989). Introduction: The changing life space of early adolescence. *Journal of Youth and Adolescence, 18,* 501–509.

Mead, G. H. (1934/1967). *Mind, self, and society: From the standpoint of a social behaviorist.* Chicago, IL: The University of Chicago Press.

Moskos, P. (2008). *Cop in the hood: My year of policing Baltimore's Eastern District.* Princeton, NJ: Princeton University Press.

National Research Council. (2004). Fairness and effectiveness in policing: The evidence. In W. Skogan & K. Frydl (Eds.), *Committee to review research on police policy and practices* (pp. 291–326). Washington, DC: The National Academies Press.

Rios, V. (2011). *Punished: Policing the lives of Black and Latino boys.* New York: New York University Press.

Rosenbaum, D. (2006). The limits of hot spot policing. In D. Weisburd & A. A. Braga (Eds.), *Policing innovation: Contrasting perspectives* (pp. 245–263). New York, NY: Cambridge University Press.

Rosenbaum, D. (2007). Police innovation post 1980: Assessing effectiveness and equity concerns in the information technology era. *IPC Review, 1*(March), 11–44.

San Francisco Violence Prevention and Intervention Unit (SFVPIU). (2011, April). *Street violence reduction initiative: San Francisco plan.* San Francisco, CA: Author. Retrieved from http://www.dcyf.org/modules/showdocument.aspx?documentid=231

Schubert, C., Hecker, T., & Losoya, S. (2004). Theory and research on desistance from antisocial activity among adolescent serious offenders. *Journal of Youth Violence and Juvenile Justice, 2,* 213–236.

Schubert, C., Mulvey, E., Steinberg, L., Cauffman, E., Losoya, S., Hecker, T., Chassin, L., & Knight, G. (2004). Operational lessons from the pathways to desistance project. *Journal of Youth Violence and Juvenile Justice, 2,* 237–255.

New Directions for Child and Adolescent Development • DOI: 10.1002/cad

Steinberg, L., & Morris, A. (2001). Adolescent development. *Annual Review of Psychology, 52*, 83–110.

Steinberg, L., Mounts, N. S., Lamborns, S. D., & Dornbusch, S. M. (1991). Authoritative parenting and adolescent adjustment across varied ecological niches. *Journal of Research on Adolescence, 1*, 19–36.

Steinberg, L., & Scott, E. (2003). Less guilty by reason of adolescence. *American Psychologist, 58*, 1–10.

Stewart, E. (2007). Either they don't know or they don't care: Black males and negative police experiences. *Criminology & Public Policy, 6*(1), 123–130.

Terrill, W. (2003). Police use of force and suspect resistance: The micro process of the police-suspect encounter. *Police Quarterly, 6*(1), 51–83.

Terrill, W., & Paoline, E. (2007). Nonarrest decision making in police-citizen encounters. *Police Quarterly, 10*(3), 308–331.

Terry v. Ohio, 392 U.S. 1 (1968). Retrieved from http://www.law.cornell.edu/supct/html/historics/USSC_CR_0392_0001_ZS.html

Tyler, T. (2006). *Why people obey the law.* Princeton, NJ: Princeton University Press.

## Notes

1. Personal names used in this chapter are pseudonyms. Brothers Changing the Hood is also a pseudonym. Research support provided by the William T. Grant Foundation.

2. In 2005, when James was in his early twenties, the *San Francisco Chronicle* described the neighborhood as the city's "deadliest" area. See Gordon (2005).

3. See Rosenbaum (2007) for a review of policing innovations since 1980. See Rosenbaum (2006) for a discussion of the limits of hot spot policing.

4. The power of police discretion is widely acknowledged in the policing literature. See Peter Moskos for a recent discussion of the use of discretion in arrests in inner-city Baltimore's drug zones (Moskos, 2008, pp. 111–157). See also Terrill and Paoline (2007).

5. See *Hiibel v. Sixth Judicial District Court of Nevada* (2004) for the U.S. Supreme Court's opinion on "reasonable suspicion."

6. The difference between a stop-and-search and a social contact is that a social or voluntary contact does not require probable cause. In such cases, an officer may initiate an encounter with a question like, "How are you doing?" or "Can I talk to you for a second?" If there is no probable cause to stop a person, the civilian can decline to stop without sanction from an officer. This is not the case if a citizen is detained, which requires, at a minimum, reasonable suspicion.

7. In some settings, there is an assembly line feel to these encounters. In such cases, groups of young men "assume the position" with little prompting from police officers who have arrived on the scene (see Brunson & Miller, 2006).

8. Several family members are named on the Western Addition gang injunction; if they do not separate the moment they walk out their front door, they are in violation of the injunction. They can be arrested, charged with a misdemeanor, and made to serve up to six months in jail.

9. Longitudinal studies of youth who commit serious felonies have found that their offending reduces over time. See Schubert, Hecker, and Losoya (2004) and Schubert et al. (2004).

NIKKI JONES *is an associate professor of African American studies at the University of California, Berkeley. E-mail: njones@berkeley.edu, webpage: betweengoodandghetto.com*

NEW DIRECTIONS FOR CHILD AND ADOLESCENT DEVELOPMENT • DOI: 10.1002/cad

Roy, K., Messina, L., Smith, J., & Waters, D. (2014). Growing up as "man of the house": Adultification and transition into adulthood for young men in economically disadvantaged families. In K. Roy & N. Jones (Eds.), *Pathways to adulthood for disconnected young men in low-income communities. New Directions in Child and Adolescent Development, 143*, 55–72.

4

# Growing Up as "Man of the House": Adultification and Transition Into Adulthood for Young Men in Economically Disadvantaged Families

*Kevin Roy, Lauren Messina, Jocelyn Smith, Damian Waters*

## Abstract

*Many children in economically disadvantaged communities assume adult roles in their families. Negotiating the responsibilities and expectations associated with becoming what some young men describe as "man of the house" has important implications for how adolescent boys move into adulthood. In this study, we share insights from field work and life-history interviews with low-income, young African American men and Salvadoran men in the Washington, DC/Baltimore region to illustrate how adultification may deliver contradictory expectations for adolescents. The findings also show how the accelerated responsibilities that accompany the experience of adultification create difficulties in the young men's transition into adulthood. These findings indicate that the age period of emerging adulthood may begin earlier for economically disadvantaged young men. © 2014 Wiley Periodicals, Inc.*

New Directions for Child and Adolescent Development, no. 143, Spring 2014 © 2014 Wiley Periodicals, Inc.
Published online in Wiley Online Library (wileyonlinelibrary.com). • DOI: 10.1002/cad.20054

55

[So what was your role in the family when you were in high school?] Man of the house. [What does that mean? What do you have to do as man of the house?] You know, I still had to ... go around the house and clean up, had to give up my room for my sister and the baby, and we only had two rooms in the apartment, had to give up my room.... A man of the house needs to do this, be caretaker, protector. Sylvester, 18

I was basically trying to be a man before I had to. Fry, 19

I was living like an adult as a kid. Matt, 20

At young ages, many children accept advanced responsibilities of provision and care for their family members, including mothers, siblings, cousins, and grandparents. Such adultification involves acquiring precocious knowledge as well as acting as peer, spouse, or even parent for one's own parents (Burton, 2007). Family transitions and movement into early adult roles (such as marriage, parenthood, or independent living) lead toward enhanced perceptions of adulthood (Johnson & Mollborn, 2009; Shanahan, Porfeli, Mortimer, & Erickson, 2005). Moreover, stress experienced through physical abuse, exposure to violence, and living in unsafe neighborhoods may result in perceptions of being older than one's age peers.

Foster, Hagan, & Brooks-Gunn (2008) examined Add Health data on young adult women and identified processes of subjective weathering, a social psychological dimension of adultification that develops alongside physical weathering related to accelerated aging due to stress (Geronimus, 1992, 2001). Few studies have examined similar processes of adultification for young men in economically disadvantaged households. Men of color face a distinct set of challenges in navigating risks in their families and communities that require them to confront institutional power, violence and trauma, and complex relationships with adults (Harding, 2010; Rich, 2009). Yet, we lack in-depth consideration of the contexts and meanings of their pathways from boyhood to adolescence and through to young adulthood.

Ethnographic and other qualitative studies provide some insight into family dynamics as young disadvantaged men age. Parents face difficult options in keeping their boys safe, monitoring their activities, and engaging them in school (Burton, Winn, Stevenson, & McKinney, 2014). Teenage boys in economically disadvantaged households may provide critical caregiving support for their siblings or financial support for their parents (Roy, Dyson, & Jackson, 2010; Roy & Smith, 2012; Roy & Vesely, 2009). Such experiences can socialize them to be involved fathers. In this way, men in disadvantaged families can play a role as kinkeepers, weaving together commitments from varied family members and promoting family legacies even as nonresidential or unmarried fathers (Burton & Stack, 2014; Marsiglio & Roy, 2012; Roy & Burton, 2007).

As Weiss (1979) noted, children in single-parent households in particular become partners in household management. Young disadvantaged men may often feel pressure to become, as one respondent describes above, "the man of the house" well before they reach their late teen years. They may seek to fill the void of an absent father who cannot play the role of man of the house. Even if they can help to manage households, care for siblings, or contribute money, boys and adolescents typically lack the authority to fulfill these adult expectations. They also receive few of the privileges afforded to parents and other adults, such as clear lines of authority, respect from other adults, or even routine privacy.

Understandings of what it means to be a man of the house reflect traditional expectations for men's patriarchal authority and responsibilities for financial provision, discipline, and decision making in family life (Coltrane, 1997; Thornton, Alwin, & Camburn, 1983). Youth develop visions that are shaped by these understandings of traditional masculine roles. Family members may use the term to compel boys to help out with their families, but these expectations can be vague and open to interpretation. These problematic expectations can lead to contradictions that have important implications for later years. Perceptions and decisions about close relationships, identity formation as a self-sufficient adult, as well as one's place in a dynamic and limited world of jobs and careers may be shaped by how young men age out of their roles as men of the house and into their own unique adulthood (Way, 2011; Young, 2004).

Adultification may carry positive consequences that emerge in young adulthood as well, as Burton (2007) indicates that some adultification processes may unfold alongside mentors. Research on emerging adulthood suggests that young adults typically seek and receive support from their parents, such as financial resources (Mouw, 2005). Even ongoing relationships with parents can provide critical social capital for young adults (Furstenberg & Hughes, 1995). Close ties may be particularly helpful to young adults at specific turning points, such as when they become parents themselves. Social support from their own parents can help to buffer new fathers from risk and keep them engaged in school and work activities (Roy, Vesely, Fitzgerald, & Buckmiller Jones, 2010).

In this study, we conducted field work and life-history interviews with low-income, young African American men and Salvadoran men in the Washington, DC/Baltimore region. Through interaction with them in community centers over many months, we explored the circumstances and contexts in which they become men of the house—or not—and how adultification may deliver contradictory sets of expectations for adolescents with few resources themselves. Most importantly, men reflected on how accelerated responsibilities and experiences shaped their own transition into a sense of adulthood. We consider conceptual contributions of these findings for our understanding of adultification and emerging adulthood for young

NEW DIRECTIONS FOR CHILD AND ADOLESCENT DEVELOPMENT • DOI: 10.1002/cad

economically disadvantaged men. Implications for policy and programs will also be discussed.

## Methods

Our research team worked for 18 months in two youth development programs in the Baltimore/Washington, DC, metropolitan area. The UP program (Urban Progress) had been situated in the community for over a decade, helping out-of-school youth and young adults to "turn their lives around." This sprawling one-story brick facility sat underneath an expressway overpass and alongside strings of rowhouses that were home to generations of African American families in the local community. UP staff provided career guidance, literacy and GED, job readiness and placement, life skills and health education classes, as well as substance abuse counseling and extensive mental health interventions and counseling. Our research team, including students trained in couple and family therapy, facilitated two weekly life skills sessions in conflict management, coping with exposure to violence, and stress and depression. Initial facilitation over 12 months was extended for another 12 months by two researchers.

The second program, Diversity Matters, was also a youth development project. In contrast, this facility was located in a former high school, tucked into the back streets of a residential community of single-family homes. A community garden ran alongside the perimeter of the building, and the facility was shared with extension educators from the nearby university. Cohorts of Diversity Matters participants worked as mentors for high school students and congregated daily in the afternoon for career training, supervision, and life skills classes. Over six months of spring/summer training, and again over the same period one year later, our research team offered similar interactive sessions in the Diversity Matters facility.

**Participants.** The UP program classes consisted of young men and women, but given the focus of our project, we approached only young men in classes to ask if they would like to participate in an interview. Twenty-one African American men, between the ages of 18 and 24, agreed to participate. The majority of these participants had lived in the local urban community since birth, among generations of family members who had grown up there as well. All of the participants had dropped out of high school, and the promise of a GED was the most important draw to the program. About 20% ($n = 4$) of the young men were fathers, and over half had some experience with incarceration in the state.

In contrast, of the 20 men recruited at the Diversity Matters site, five were African American, two were West African, and 13 were Salvadoran, which reflected the racial and ethnic variation in the program as a whole. They tended to be younger than the participants from the UP site (17–19 years) and in their first two years after high school graduation, another contrast to the UP participants. Most of these young men lived in immigrant families, as first- or second-generation immigrants, and were the first members of their families to aspire to go to college. As a group, their families were a mix of working-class and low-income households. None of them were young parents, and only a few were considered ex-offenders.

We planned to recruit two groups of young men with these subtle but important differences in educational attainment. Variation by age, race, and ethnicity was also important in understanding processes of adultification and parental support, and we hoped to capture different family household configurations as well. An emergent and unexpected theme was a consideration of being or becoming a man of the house, and as a result, we purposively sought to speak with young men who had this experience as adolescents or boys. When we reached close to 20 participants in each site, we realized that we had multiple cases of being a man of the house, as well as rich variation in the meaning and circumstances behind this status. There were also many cases in which young men were not expected to jump into accelerated adult roles, and these young men provide a helpful contrast group.

**Data Collection.** We used two primary methods of data collection. For many weeks, the research team took extensive field notes on formal session interactions as well as informal and extended conversations with staff and participants in each site. This method provided information on ecological processes and contexts (such as negotiation of neighborhoods and peer networks, limited job and educational opportunities, and physical mobility), community barriers and supports for youth development, mental health considerations (especially from the UP site), and close relationships with friends and family members. After we developed a consistent and trusting relationship with the participants, we mentioned to each of the young men in class that we would like to arrange an interview with them. We worked to approach each class member, but those who did not attend regularly were less likely to be approached multiple times for an interview. They also were less likely to confirm and meet for an interview, even after initial agreement.

We met young men in a separate, private classroom in each site to conduct a one- to two-hour interview. These semistructured life-history interviews examined how family members, primarily parents and close kin, supported sons in the transition into adulthood. The semistructured format provided a general guide for the questions that interviewers asked while allowing them flexibility to further explore aspects of participant's experiences in taking on adult-like responsibilities as children and adolescents (Daly, 2007). We asked participants to discuss their daily routines, next steps for work and education, support networks of friends and family, school and job experiences, what it meant to be an adult, and when their families first considered them to be adults. In many interviews, we also discussed family conflict (such as divorce or domestic violence), immigration and fluid residential or custodial change, coming to terms with masculinity and manhood, intimate relationships, incarceration and gang activity, and depression or related trauma. We should note that we never asked explicitly about the young men playing the role of man of the house; this term was used by participants to illustrate their personal understanding of the range of adult responsibilities that they assumed at a young age.

We also used a range of methods to enhance the trustworthiness of data (Lincoln & Guba, 1985). Credibility and dependability of the data were enhanced by use of multiple sources of data and multiple methods of data collection, as well as prolonged engagement in the field. In-person discussions with the majority of the young men some weeks after their interviews (i.e., member checks) were used to check our understanding of how their experiences as adolescents in their families shaped their own views and expectations of being adults. Interviews were recorded on audiotapes and transcribed, and interview and field note texts were coded using AtlasTI software. Pseudonyms were used for participants.

**Data Analysis.** Following grounded theory, analysis occurs over three phases of coding: open, axial, and selective (LaRossa, 2005). Open coding, the first phase of analysis, refers to a "line-by-line" breakdown of the interview data (Daly, 2007). The researchers developed a set of sensitizing concepts from existing studies of disadvantaged young men and emerging adulthood, including adultification (and its dimensions), generativity, turning points, cool pose, coping strategies, socialization, soft skills, micro aggressions, and aspirations/expectations. We also began to discover emergent codes based on themes described by young men. These included the process of ghosting, or disappearing from school, work, family, and friends for set periods of time, and man of the house, as we discuss in this analysis.

Axial coding involved identifying conceptually similar categories while noting the overlapping and distinguishing characteristics of the codes. Working across 41 cases, we explored variation in specific codes. For example, participants were initially given the title man of the house after a range of specific events, such as departure of their fathers, their mothers' loss of a job, or bringing home money for the first time. We examined differences across each site, and by cultural context. Moreover, we found that some parents stepped back to let their sons perform adult duties; others carefully extended these duties step by step; and a few never asked their sons to take on accelerated responsibilities in care or provision. Finally, during a wave of selective coding, we conceptually linked together major and minor codes to offer a full and detailed framework of how being a man of the house shaped perceptions and even decisions about the transition into adulthood. This coding required following several cases throughout the analysis as well as summarizing three broad themes that reflected differences both within individual men's experiences and across them as groups.

New Directions for Child and Adolescent Development • DOI: 10.1002/cad

## Findings

Among the young men in the youth development programs, the large majority had experienced forms of accelerated adulthood as boys and adolescents. Almost three quarters ($n = 30$, 73%) of the men noted that they acted "like an adult" by contributing financially, caring for family members, or confronting challenges that required higher levels of maturity, including violence, substance use, or extensive self-care. Only 11 of the young men (27% of the group) stated that their parents had worked to take them step by step into adult responsibilities, in line with their age and maturity.

Not all of the 30 young men who encountered adult-like challenges would be considered men of the house, however. Seven of these young men spent extensive time alone as adolescents, without parental supervision and without responsibility for anyone but themselves. Over half of the entire sample ($n = 23$, 56%) were considered men of the house, indicated through direct reference during interviews or through interpretation by coders of the interview data.

For an adolescent or even a boy, a man of the house assumed responsibilities for family members, which could include his mother, father, siblings, cousins, or close kin. He may find a job and bring money home; he may cook dinner and dress younger children; he may supervise his siblings for days at a time, in the absence of older adults. A critical window onto the role of being man of the house was each young man's relationship with his mother. For some, man of the house was a role conferred by his single mother, in need of a partner for financial, caregiving, or even emotional support. Some adolescents took on this role despite disagreements and conflict with their mothers.

In the following sections, we explore three themes that emerged in our analyses. First, there were a range of clear family transitions that initiated boys and adolescents into early adult responsibilities. Second, as they struggled to fulfill expectations as men of the house, these young men faced a cluster of contradictions, confusion, and risks to their own health and well-being. Finally, they interpreted next steps into adulthood through their understanding of "being adults already," as one respondent explained. Often they noticed how vague responsibilities they had assumed as boys or early adolescents seldom translated well in adulthood, when they were called to earn money to support themselves or to care for their own children.

**Early Family Transitions Initiate Young Men Into Adult Responsibilities.** During times of stressful transitions during their childhood or early adolescence, participants discovered that their families needed extra help, substitute supervision, and a handful of additional resources to bolster limited dollars at the end of the week. Men noted that during these transitions, family turned to them, or alternatively, responsibilities seemed to fall into their laps. Such transitions often did not unfold quickly, but took many months to play out in family routines. One

NEW DIRECTIONS FOR CHILD AND ADOLESCENT DEVELOPMENT • DOI: 10.1002/cad

young man, Empire, insisted that "I'm gonna be one wise person when I get older." He insisted that he learned to "block out the periphery," to deal with stress and confusion in his life, because "I was raised with old people, I was raised sitting there listening to things that I'm not supposed to be listening to."

The departure of their own fathers from the household, or their inadequate fulfillment of the provider role, often became the presumption that the next-oldest male—whatever his age—might take on the title of man of the house. Whereas some participants were thrust into the role suddenly after fathers departed abruptly (i.e., due to death, dissolution of the couple relationship), others began enacting the role more gradually while their fathers were present but not contributing fully.

Fry was a young unemployed man in East Baltimore who realized on his own, at an early age, that his father was not living up to his family responsibilities. Although his father lived at home and even went to work, an unspoken assumption—and a growing notion in his own understanding—was that something was missing:

> He was the type that he really do for himself, he'll steal from his own family, his sisters and stuff like that. It's like he really don't care, like he's in it for himself. I just started realizing when I was, like, 11 or 12, damn, he ain't really doing nothing. I see why we keep having to move from here to here, there to here. See, when you young, you looking at it like, "well, daddy, he get up and go to work everyday" but you not knowing what is going on under the table. He get up and go to work everyday but he not bringing no money home whatsoever. He not putting no food in the house.

At this age, Fry began to look for odd jobs to pay for food for his siblings and himself. He had very limited understanding of the lack of work opportunities for adult men in the city, or the experiences that led his own father to disengage and to sink into depression. But his own entry into adulthood was closely linked to the failure of his own father to be a responsible adult. Similarly, Sylvester, an 18-year-old young man who dropped out of his high school in Baltimore, asserted that he became an adult, a man of the house, "when my father left." He could not recall when the departure happened; to him, he had been man of the house, "like, forever, as long as I can remember."

Relationships between mothers and their sons were deeply affected by the need for a man of the house. Single mothers looked to their sons for input about household decisions, as confidantes and protectors. And young men's relationships with their mothers often were transformed simply by witnessing hardship and conflict. For example, Matt, a 20-year-old father of two children, had served multiple sentences and had survived multiple injuries, including trauma from many years of gang activity. As a boy, he watched his father and mother fight hand to hand. "My mother left my father; I didn't care," he said. "That ain't nothing. I see that every day for real so that ain't bother me." He spent a handful of years as a boy, working alongside his mother to keep their household intact, but by the age of 15 he had left home and fathered his own child.

The young men occupied a position of authority while their mothers were away from the home but reverted to a more deferential position when mothers were present. Typically, they became the "adult" in charge of younger children when their mothers worked. However, their roles might deepen considerably when mothers hit rough patches in their own employment. De'Onte, a 17-year-old young man, was the youngest of three children, with two older sisters. He watched his best friend get shot and killed at the age of 4, "and I would just cry and walk in the house or go to sleep because of what I saw that day." He never knew his father, but he did remember "living with nothing...no TV, not eating meat for a whole year. That was amazing—how could I survive without meat?" De'Onte's mother was fired from her job at the post office, and his family lived off of unemployment and social security benefits. At the age of nine, he reassured her, "Mommy, we're getting out of [the projects], don't worry...alright, I'm gonna find a job."

Some men assumed responsibilities for their family members despite their mothers' resistance to their newfound authority. A young Salvadoran high school graduate, Emani, definitely was not a partner with his mother in household management. He reminded her of his biological father, a Guatemalan laborer who left her prior to Emani's birth. To him, years of resentment had created a tolerance of his presence, but little closeness to his mother. However, at six years old, he confronted his mother's brother, who attempted to assault Emani's sister:

> I tried to stop him and stuff, but I wasn't strong enough. He overpowered me, beat me down pretty hard, but we got him arrested....And then my family went mad, they all ended up chipping in to put bail for him. So that's why I always, you know, I wasn't very close to them.

Although he kept his distance from adults in his family, Emani threw himself into caring for his sisters and cousins. He was known, it seemed, as the emotional center of his family and his group of peers.

Some young men discussed a long history of living apart from their families, of growing up "on my own." Mike was a 23 year old who was kicked out of school the last few weeks of his senior year, after he and his girlfriend got into trouble in the neighborhood. His father had died when Mike was 15, and his mother passed away when he was 21. At the time of our interview, he had started a temporary job at Target, but had been kicked out of his aunt's apartment. Mike had little to say about being a man of the house; he recalled few days in his family home and had few opportunities to try out adult responsibilities.

NEW DIRECTIONS FOR CHILD AND ADOLESCENT DEVELOPMENT • DOI: 10.1002/cad

Finally, as we discussed above, about a quarter of the entire group of participants lived with their parents who worked diligently to scaffold experiences in ways that were appropriate for their age and maturity. Although they grew up in the same neighborhoods and schools as other participants, these young men did not deal with inappropriate adult responsibilities or confusing knowledge about conflict or relationships. Eugene was a 19-year-old high school graduate at the Diversity Matters program, and he discussed working with his father on his first job at 13 years old. His family formed a supportive "Team Gene, so I'm happy," and by his account, they had high expectations for him as a middle child because they knew he could succeed. Although he dropped out of high school in tenth grade, Kuron, a 17 year old in the UP program, lived with both of his parents. They stuck by him to study and earn his GED, and he looked forward to doing more things as a family, "like when we used to go to church." These young men's experiences seemed in marked contrast to the rush of responsibilities that many of their peers had to absorb on a daily basis.

**Contradictory Expectations Place Risks on Men of the House.** Participants assumed adult responsibilities at different ages, and families' expectations expanded as they matured, gained greater capacities, and access to resources. But as boys and early adolescents, they encountered contradictory expectations from their families, communities, and larger society. Although being men of the house could train them for self-sufficiency and socialize them to successful adulthood, it was more likely to overwhelm these young men who could become confused and put their own health and well-being at risk trying to live up to accelerated expectations.

In the absence of their mothers or other adults, many boys and adolescents were asked to manage households. They allocated space to siblings, took charge of cleaning, and delegated household tasks to other family members. These management tasks could prove difficult in small apartments with few resources, but their roles were vital to keeping families fed and on-task. As Sylvester discussed his experiences managing household resources above, he noted that he "had to go around the house and clean up." He even made the executive decision to move out of his room—"to throw the bed out and everything"—that he shared with his sister, as a sacrifice to make room for his niece, who needed a place to stay. For Sylvester, the distinctions between managing his household, taking care of younger children, and protecting them were unclear. Such responsibilities merged and resurfaced depending on what was needed on a particular day. Similarly, for Justin, a young man in East Baltimore, caretaking involved not only checking in on his siblings, but soon his mother's well-being as well. His mental checklist was as extensive as many parents' checklists:

> [And what was your role in the family? Did you have responsibilities when you were 11 or 12?] Psssh ... um ... being the man of the house and keeping my brothers and sisters in order, help moms out. [When you say man of the

house, how did you do that?] Make sure the house is cleaned up, make sure they're in bed in time. You know, food get cooked, help served the plates and everything. Help out with the homework and everything. You know, make sure the trash is took out, floor is mopped and swept. Bathrooms and all of that, make sure the door is locked. Make sure everybody has their night clothes. And you know, make sure my work was done and make sure moms is good and get up the next morning and go to school. Checked on her, you know, ask her how her day was ... do you need anything before I go to bed and stuff like that.

Young men allocated their own time, space, and limited resources to meet the needs of other members of their families, even if that means personal sacrifice. In addition to managing household resources, they often provided financially for their families, even at very young ages. De'Onte, in his pledge to move his mother out of the projects, began to play music at church at nine years old. He brought home his first paycheck of $500, and he came home in tears—and his mother sat and cried as well. From that moment, "we've been moving on up!" as partners who shared responsibility for their family's well-being. He also washed clothes, cooked, cleaned, and did yard work ("now that we have a back yard"). Although this was an exceptional circumstance, many young men discussed bringing home money when they could find occasional hours as day laborers that paid cash-in-hand.

While some young men were able to earn money through formal employment, their relative youth limited mainstream job opportunities. As an alternative, young men turned to engagement in illegal activities. Fry began selling drugs to provide for his family when his father failed to do so. Although their families needed their financial contributions, Fry's story illustrates that young men may pay the heavy price of incarceration, injury, or death as they aim to help their families:

[I] was the so-called provider in my family because I seen that my father wasn't doing it. So, I felt like because I was the next man in line and I was home, it was my job to be. That's really made me want to get out there and want to sell drugs and want to hustle. And that's really got me in a position to get locked up and my little brother says like, we need clothes, shoes, all that. . . . That's responsibility.

To complicate his role as man of the house, Fry's commitment to earn money placed his mother in a difficult situation. She knew that he brought home "dirty money," and she argued that "it ain't good money if it's dirty money, even though the money was helping her." He asserted that he was being a man, placing responsibility for his family in front of all else— although Fry's mother was torn by placing her son at great risk:

She had no other choice because she understood where I was coming from. I was basically trying to be a man before I had to. There was no other alternative unless you want to be sitting out on the streets and that's not what we wanted. I wasn't really trying to hear her because my main focus was providing for my family. I mean a lot of my life experience came from me worrying about the next person. Well, I can't say the next person because they not just anybody. I was worrying about my family.

Men who were committed to earning money—and could do so—were tough to find in these neighborhoods, and some found that their family commitments could multiply quickly, even at a young age. Matt had split bills with his mother when he was 15, and "she didn't want me doing that." Like Fry, he pushed past his mother's resistance and stressed to her that "she couldn't be mad at me because all of my kids were taken care of, she was taken care of, her bill was taken care of, I was taken care of." His ability to pay for her daily expenses, as well as himself and his young son's needs, is an impressive accomplishment for an adolescent. In effect, Matt was a man of the house twice over, although hustling eventually led to his arrest and took him out of these homes—leaving his infant son and his own mother at even greater risk.

Further, some young men were abruptly pushed out of their roles as man of the house by the entry of older males into their lives. After serving as a pseudopartner for their single mothers for years during adolescence, they were stunned to find their mothers' boyfriends move into their homes and challenge their hard-won authority. These older men forced the young men to renegotiate their management tasks or their ability to make decisions about cooking, cleaning, and care. Emani, for example, was pulled into numerous fist fights with his stepfather, who insisted that "there isn't any room for another man in this house" and tried his best to move the young man out of the house when he turned 18. Apart from losing respect and authority, relationships with their mothers became much more tenuous. They were no longer junior partners with the presence of actual (or potential) household partners, and the companionship that they shared with their mothers—although it may have been developmentally questionable at times—often dissolved in the transition into adulthood as a result.

**Difficult Transition Into Adulthood Is a Consequence of Adultification.** When we discussed how they felt about being an adult—or if they considered themselves to be adults—participants had clear opinions, but often unsettled identities. Their confrontations with challenges such as family conflict, violence, or emotional concerns that would burden adults many times their own age seemed to shape how they saw themselves. In part, the disjuncture between accelerated adulthood status as men of the house, and the inability to move toward successful adulthood status as self-sufficient workers and family men, was jarring.

NEW DIRECTIONS FOR CHILD AND ADOLESCENT DEVELOPMENT • DOI: 10.1002/cad

Kevin, a 19-year-old African American GED student, lived with his father and struggled to simply take care of his own needs:

> I became an adult when I started working with my father, two years ago. I used to buy my own food, buy my own clothes, pay my phone bill. You're gonna play the Grown Ass Man however you want to pay. And if you like my age, like eighteen, or if you're sixteen, and you take care of yourself then you one of them.

Sylvester, who felt that he'd been an adult "forever," faced the complications of becoming a man and how he almost fooled himself into believing that he would not have to prove himself repeatedly, and in challenging ways, as he aged:

> I always said I'm an old man because I got respect, ever since I grew up, I always did the right thing...I call myself a fool now, but, cause I preach to my friends now, they say always preaching cause I try to get people on the right track. I'd do for somebody before I do myself, you feel me, try to help somebody else before I help myself. But when I got older it was like I wanted for myself, but at the same time I got to for the family as well, so that's when I start trying to go out, without no jobs, trying to get my own money. Now it's like, eighteen now, and them books aren't for everybody, you feel me.

The realities of getting a college degree or finding a good job proved daunting to Sylvester, as to many young men in disadvantaged communities. As benchmarks of successful adulthood, they seemed unattainable, and starkly separated from the experiences of adolescence that had seemingly prepared them to step up as adults. Why couldn't they take care of themselves after they had taken care of other family members when they were so young?

In the face of the barriers to school and work, families encouraged young men to at least put on the appearance of being responsible and engaged with making progress. Snoop, a 17-year-old high school dropout, acknowledged the importance of public perception as he moved into adulthood:

> My peoples want to see you doing good, they want to see you like you got to have your shit looking good. You gotta be basically a clean cut dude, can't be no raggedy dude. You can be a man and still be like raggedy for real but you still you know got your priorities straight. They just want to see you feeling better about yourself for real, they want to see you step your level up a little bit, you got a good paying job and you go to school and start looking good. They want you to be a good role model to any other young man or woman in our family.

NEW DIRECTIONS FOR CHILD AND ADOLESCENT DEVELOPMENT • DOI: 10.1002/cad

Although these expectations seemed basic enough, they were quite daunting for young men. Few men in their own families had achieved stability as role models, and it was risky for young men to make moves toward successful adult achievements for fear of failure.

These young men realized that they could not achieve adulthood on their own, and many turned repeatedly to their own parents for help in the transition. In doing so, they faced up to generations of loss and pain in job loss, broken relationships, or strained relationships with parents. At 17, Stefan had a two-year-old son who was moved to Georgia, but he was committed to earning his GED after leaving school in eighth grade. He lived with his father, which set him apart from the large majority of young men in these two programs. Stefan had to convince his father, as well as himself, that he was ready to become an adult:

> How am I going to make my own decisions, if I'm always depend on my father? Well I've been at that stage for a while. But I've tried to keep a lot of it in. But now as I'm getting older it's starting to come out more. My father's start to see it but he's taking it the wrong way. He's taking it as disrespect when it's not disrespect it's just me wanting to choose thing for myself, wanting to do things on my own. Now, he's, uhh, recently, he's finally just listened to me. I didn't let him have it but I said, "Listen I'm not disrespected you I'm just getting older." I said, "I know your father passed away and you never had that time to grow out from under your father's shell. How every guy's gotta grow out from under his father, I'm here to show you how it looks. I'm not here to disrespect you dad, but I'm showing you now."

For those with limited support from and no regular contact with family members, early experiences of adultification could lead young men to isolate themselves from family and friends. They could not commit to exploring work and school until they examined who they might become as adults in a society with few spaces for them. They "ghosted" through daily routines that did not put them "at risk" while at the same time "being a risk" to family and friends. Emani still did not know "what comes next." He lived a few nights each week with his mother and stepfather, but left the house when his mother woke up for work. Other nights he spent sleeping outside or on a friend's couch. Joseph, a young mentor in the Diversity Matters program, also couch-surfed among three different residences, unable to tell us where he might spend the next night. He had not spoken with his parents in many months, and at 18 years old, he had entered into a "gray period" to do "a lot of thinking about what comes next." At 20, Matt looked back on the birth of his two children, his incarceration and physical injuries, and how his efforts to provide and care had led him to be wary of trusting friends or family:

I don't trust anyone. I ain't getting into trouble, not going to jail, none of that. Having a child gave me a humbleness and all that. Don't have new freedoms as an adult. I was living like an adult as a kid.

In contrast, the small number of young men who did not experience adultification could also point to efforts that their families might make to scaffold a series of next steps into actual adulthood. On working-class wages, without their own college or high school education, their parents sacrificed and hoped each day that their sons could move past the years of risk that young adulthood promised. Brandon, an 18-year-old Salvadoran mentor outside of Washington, DC, aspired to own a restaurant. He worked hard as a busboy and landed three different jobs that kept him working 30 hours on top of his high school schedule. He laughed as he recounted his parents' efforts to urge him toward adulthood:

I don't want to be called old. My parents would call me a young man. Does that count? Like she tells me "you can sometimes make like your own decisions and choices now so you need to be careful out in this world now." I guess, she'll consider me pretty much an adult once I graduate in June. So she knows I'll make the right decision, cause I've been doing it for a while. Bit by bit they're starting to pull back now. Like, well, with the whole job thing, the fact that I got the job is because they want me to use my own money to get what I want instead of me asking them all the time "get me this, get me that." And they want me to understand that, you need to earn it, so I feel comfortable with that.

## Discussion

In communities of economically disadvantaged families, the transition into adulthood becomes a process of life course negotiation for young men who struggle to fit into settings that have only limited places for them as adults. First, we found that boys and early adolescents were recruited into the role of man of the house during critical family turning points. These included the departure of their fathers from their households, or their fathers' failures as providers; the movement of their mothers to full-time employment, or the loss of such a job; depression, stress, or other mental health concerns for their parents; or even the addition of multiple younger siblings or related kin, who overwhelmed caregiving capacity for adults in their families.

Second, in the rush to encourage these boys and adolescents to become men of the house, expectations for care and provision were often vague, confusing, and contradictory. For example, many were expected to manage households with little money or social support, which were tasks that would thwart most grown adults. In turn, men of the house sought and usually failed to find substantial resources through mainstream activities—like a

NEW DIRECTIONS FOR CHILD AND ADOLESCENT DEVELOPMENT • DOI: 10.1002/cad

full-time job. Many turned to activities like hustling that presented risks to their own health and well-being.

Finally, they interpreted next steps into adulthood through their understanding of "being adults already," as one respondent explained. Being adultified resulted in a confusing and complicated transition into actual adulthood. Often they noticed how responsibilities they had assumed as boys or early adolescents seldom translated well into adulthood. Being self-sufficient at 21 was quite different from contributing cash to the household at 13; solo caregiving for siblings for a handful of hours paled in comparison to daily involvement with one's children.

These findings echo prior research which finds that pseudomaturity or real maturity depends largely on family and community contexts (Galambos, Kolaric, Sears, & Maggs, 1999), not simply on individual traits or subjective perceptions. It is an in-depth understanding of these social contexts that offer a glimpse of the underlying mechanisms that sustain the impact of adultification. The urgent needs of families living in poverty may exacerbate the experience of adultification. And complicated and fluid family relationships, in which boys and adolescents step in for their fathers or step out as mothers' partners contest their accelerated authority, may further solidify the importance of being an adult. Poverty and family relationships as well as the timing of adultification each shape an emergent sense of self for boys and early adolescents. They carry this sense of self, this adult identity, ahead for many years, well into their own transition into adulthood.

In addition to identifying problems for disconnected young adults, we need to identify processes that foster connections to adult roles. Social support can be critical for children and adolescents, and we assume that it is also critical for successful transition into adult roles. But research is limited about the processes and contexts of such support. Moreover, economically disadvantaged men of color have been marginalized by policies that regulate their presence in dynamic and complex family households for decades (Cross-Barnet, Cherlin, & Burton, 2011; Lefkowitz, 2011).

Taking into account the early life experiences of young men as they step up to take on adult-like responsibilities, social policy and programs might offer clear and systemic pathways into school and work for disadvantaged youth (Edelman, Holzer, & Offner, 2006; Mincy, 2006). Further, sustained efforts to redress poverty and inequality in general will potentially relieve young children of the burdens they now assume to support their own families, with the payoff seen years later, in their substantial achievements as adults.

Research support provided by the William T. Grant Foundation.

## References

Burton, L. (2007). Childhood adultification in economically disadvantaged families: A conceptual model. *Family Relations, 56,* 329–354.

Burton, L., & Stack, C. (2014). "Breakfast at Elmo's": Adolescent boys, slow ethnography, and disruptive politics in the kinscripts' narrative. In M. Nelson, A. Garey, & R. Hertz (Eds.), *Open to disruption: Time and craft in the practice of slow sociology.* Nashville, TN: Vanderbilt University Press.

Burton, L., Winn, D., Stevenson, H., & McKinney, M. (2014). Childhood adultification and the paradox of parenting: Perspectives on African American boys in economically-disadvantaged families. In J. Arditti (Ed.), *Family problems: Stress, risk, & resilience.* New York, NY: Wiley Blackwell.

Coltrane, S. (1997). *Family man: Fatherhood, housework, and gender equity.* New York, NY: Oxford University Press.

Cross-Barnet, C., Cherlin, A., & Burton, L. (2011). Bound by children: Intermittent cohabitation and living together apart. *Family Relations, 60,* 633–647.

Daly, K. (2007). *Qualitative methods for family studies and human development.* Thousand Oaks, CA: Sage.

Edelman, P., Holzer, H., & Offner, P. (2006). *Reconnecting disadvantaged young men.* Washington, DC: Urban Institute Press.

Foster, H., Hagan, J., & Brooks-Gunn, J. (2008). Growing up fast: Stress exposure and subjective "weathering" in emerging adulthood. *Journal of Health and Social Behavior, 49,* 162–177.

Furstenberg, F., & Hughes, M. (1995). Social capital and successful development among at-risk youth. *Journal of Marriage and Family, 57,* 580–592.

Galambos, N., Kolaric, G., Sears, H., & Maggs, J. (1999). Adolescents' subjective age: An indicator of perceived maturity. *Journal of Research on Adolescence, 9,* 309–337.

Geronimus, A. (1992). The weathering hypothesis and the health of African-American women and infants: Evidence and speculations. *Ethnicity & Disease, 2,* 207–221.

Geronimus, A. (2001). Understanding and eliminating racial inequalities in women's health in the United States: The role of the weathering conceptual framework. *Journal of the American Medical Women's Association, 56,* 133–136, 149–150.

Harding, D. (2010). *Living the drama: Community, conflict, and culture among inner-city boys.* Chicago, IL: University of Chicago Press.

Johnson, M. K., & Mollborn, S. (2009). Growing up faster, feeling older: Hardship in childhood and adolescence. *Social Psychology Quarterly, 72,* 39–60.

LaRossa, R. (2005). Grounded theory methods and qualitative family research. *Journal of Marriage and Family, 67,* 837–857.

Lefkowitz, A. (2011). Men in the house: Race, welfare, and the regulation of men's sexuality in the United States, 1961–1972. *Journal of the History of Sexuality, 20,* 594–614.

Lincoln, Y., & Guba, E. (1985). *Naturalistic inquiry.* Thousand Oaks, CA: Sage.

Marsiglio, W., & Roy, K. (2012). *Nurturing dads: Social initiatives for contemporary fatherhood.* ASA Rose Series. New York, NY: Russell Sage Foundation.

Mincy, R. (Ed.). (2006). *Black males left behind.* Washington, DC: Urban Institute Press.

Mouw, T. (2005). Sequences of early adult transitions: A look at variability and consequences. In R. A. Settersten, Jr., F. F. Furstenberg, Jr., & R. G. Rumbaut (Eds.), *On the frontier of adulthood: Theory, research, and public policy* (pp. 256–291). Chicago, IL: University of Chicago Press.

Rich, J. (2009). *Wrong place, wrong time: Trauma and violence in the lives of young Black men.* Baltimore, MD: Johns Hopkins University Press.

Roy, K., & Burton, L. (2007). Mothering through recruitment: Kinscription of non-residential fathers and father figures in low-income families. *Family Relations, 56,* 24–39.

Roy, K., Dyson, O., & Jackson, J. (2010). Intergenerational support and reciprocity between low-income African American fathers and their aging mothers. In W. Johnson & E. Johnson (Eds.), *Social work with African American males* (pp. 42–60). New York, NY: Oxford University Press.

NEW DIRECTIONS FOR CHILD AND ADOLESCENT DEVELOPMENT • DOI: 10.1002/cad

Roy, K., & Smith, J. (2012). Nonresident fathers and intergenerational parenting in kin networks. In N. Cabrera & C. Tamis-LeMonda (Eds.), *Handbook of father involvement: Multidisciplinary perspectives* (2nd ed., pp. 320–337). New York, NY: Routledge.

Roy, K., & Vesely, C. (2009). Caring for "the family's child": Social capital and kin networks of young low-income African American fathers. In R. Coles & C. Green (Eds.), *The myth of the missing Black father* (pp. 215–240). New York, NY: Columbia University Press.

Roy, K., Vesely, C., Fitzgerald, M., & Buckmiller Jones, N. (2010). Young fathers at work: The influence of parental closeness and contact on employment. *Research on Human Development, 7*, 123–139.

Shanahan, M., Porfeli, E., Mortimer, J., & Erickson, L. (2005). Subjective age identity and the transition to adulthood. In R. Settersten, F. Furstenberg, & R. Rumbaut (Eds.), *On the frontier of adulthood: Theory, research, and public policy* (pp. 225–255). Chicago, IL: University of Chicago Press.

Thornton, A., Alwin, D., & Camburn, D. (1983). Causes and consequences of sex role attitudes and attitude change. *American Sociological Review, 48*, 211–227.

Way, N. (2011). *Deep secrets: Boys' friendships and the crisis of connection.* Cambridge, MA: Harvard University Press.

Weiss, R. (1979). Growing up a little faster: The experience of growing up in a single parent household. *Journal of Social Issues, 35*, 97–111.

Young, A. (2004). *The minds of marginalized Black men: Making sense of mobility, opportunity, and future life chances.* Princeton, NJ: Princeton University Press.

KEVIN ROY *is an associate professor in the Department of Family Science, School of Public Health at the University of Maryland, College Park. E-mail:  kroy@umd.edu,  webpage:  http://www.sph.umd.edu/fmsc/people/fac/kroy.html*

LAUREN MESSINA *is a doctoral student in the Department of Family Science at the University of Maryland. E-mail: lauren.messina@gmail.com*

JOCELYN SMITH *is the Paul B. Cornely Postdoctoral Scholar and Research Fellow at the University of Michigan. E-mail: jrsmith11@gmail.com*

DAMIAN WATERS *is a doctoral student in the Department of Family Science at the University of Maryland. E-mail: dmw23georgetown@gmail.com*

NEW DIRECTIONS FOR CHILD AND ADOLESCENT DEVELOPMENT • DOI: 10.1002/cad

Settersten, R. A., Jr., Day, J. K., Cancel-Tirado, D., & Driscoll, D. M. (2014). Fathers' accounts of struggle and growth in early adulthood: An exploratory study of disadvantaged men. In K. Roy & N. Jones (Eds.), *Pathways to adulthood for disconnected young men in low-income communities. New Directions in Child and Adolescent Development, 143*, 73–89.

5

# Fathers' Accounts of Struggle and Growth in Early Adulthood: An Exploratory Study of Disadvantaged Men

*Richard A. Settersten, Jr., Jack K. Day,*
*Doris Cancel-Tirado, Debra Minar Driscoll*

## Abstract

*This chapter explores how fatherhood prompts struggle and growth in the psychological, social, and economic changes associated with the transition to adulthood. Little is known about these connections, especially for disadvantaged Latino and White fathers who live in small and mid-sized American communities. We draw on eight in-depth focus groups with 48 fathers (27 Latino and 21 White) who have children in low-income schools in a small and mid-sized American community. These men face significant challenges in establishing themselves at work—a central task of both adulthood and fatherhood—and in balancing these demands alongside the strong expectation that they also be involved fathers. Involved fathering is key to understanding dynamics related to identity and meaning and to relationships with spouses and friends, which are also intertwined with the process of becoming adult. The discussion considers how fatherhood can promote and constrain adult development for disadvantaged men. © 2014 Wiley Periodicals, Inc.*

How do disadvantaged men view the impact of fatherhood on their early adult lives? This chapter explores how fatherhood prompts struggle and growth for disadvantaged men in the psychological, social, and economic changes associated with the transition to adulthood.

Becoming a parent has traditionally been considered one of the five primary social roles that mark entry into adulthood—alongside leaving home, finishing school, getting work, and finding a spouse or partner (e.g., Settersten, Furstenberg, & Rumbaut, 2005). Parenthood is now viewed as an experience that culminates the process of becoming adult rather than one that starts it, especially in the middle class (Furstenberg, 2010; Settersten & Ray, 2010). Partner and parent roles are also increasingly being decoupled from notions of adulthood (Settersten, 2012; Spéder, Murinkó, & Settersten, 2014).

Experiences in early adult life are inherently different depending on whether or when one becomes a parent. While the median age of parenthood has increased for all social classes, young men from disadvantaged backgrounds, or who are engaged in risky behavior, remain more likely to enter parenthood before reaching other adult milestones, such as completing education or finding stable employment, which brings a host of negative outcomes (Cherlin, 2010; Dariotis, Pleck, Astone, & Sonenstein, 2011; Pears, Pierce, Kim, Capaldi, & Owen, 2005). Men who are disadvantaged as they make their way into adulthood may therefore be further disadvantaged by fatherhood. They are also much less likely to be involved fathers (Hofferth & Goldscheider, 2010) and to coreside with children (Goldscheider, Hofferth, Spearin, & Curtin, 2009).

At the same time, becoming a father may also lead some disadvantaged men to increase their commitment to work (e.g., Astone, Dariotis, Sonenstein, Pleck, & Hynes, 2010; Dew & Eggebeen, 2010; Roy, Vesely, Fitzgerald, & Buckmiller Jones, 2010) and their connections to community and extended family members (e.g., Duckworth & Buzzanell, 2009). In these cases, fatherhood instead might represent a discontinuous break from a negative past, becoming a kind of positive turning point in a man's life (Kerr, Capaldi, Owen, Wiesner, & Pears, 2011; Sampson & Laub, 2005). This serves as a reminder that fatherhood is not a discrete event but rather a long-term process that is embedded in a larger developmental trajectory as men make their way into adulthood (Eggebeen, Knoester, & McDaniel, 2013; Palkovitz & Palm, 2009; Settersten & Cancel-Tirado, 2010).

## Parenting and Men's Development and Identity in Young Adulthood

Recent psychological research suggests that young men and women no longer frame their sense of adulthood in terms of traditional markers, such as partnering and parenting, but instead favor more abstract and individualistic criteria. For example, achieving a state of "maturity" is conceptualized

NEW DIRECTIONS FOR CHILD AND ADOLESCENT DEVELOPMENT • DOI: 10.1002/cad

as taking responsibility for oneself, making independent decisions, and becoming financially independent (Arnett, 2000), or to developing other individualized senses of psychological maturity (Côté, 2000).

And yet, maturity is also likely to be facilitated by the roles of partner and parent. For example, some degree of maturity is required to be effective in these roles—and, indeed, there is evidence that many young people are now actively postponing marriage and parenthood precisely because they want to be ready for and do well in these roles (Settersten, 2011). At the same time, maturity can grow from the responsibilities demanded by partnering and parenting. Once individuals have entered these roles, they often look back on them as pivotal and transformative events in their own development; this is especially true of parenthood because it entails responsibility for the welfare of a fragile and dependent human being (Settersten, 2011). Similarly, fatherhood might facilitate some of the other social or economic milestones that are associated with the transition to adulthood—such as stronger attachment to the labor market or more positive family and social relationships.

While the notion of "adulthood" is often equated with "independence" in the United States, this emphasis is ironic because individuals seldom operate autonomously as they move through adulthood. This is particularly apparent when it comes to marriage and parenthood, which bring social ties that deepen not only life's meanings and joys but also its hardships, and that determine much of who we become and what we are able to do. In this sense, *inter*dependence is probably more accurately the hallmark of adult life (Settersten, 2012). A mature perspective on relationships comes with the important realization that while commitments to others place constraints on individual freedom and choice, they can also be associated with happiness and life satisfaction.

Becoming a father means confronting these tensions if men are to meet expectations that they be both good providers and involved fathers (Kaufman & Uhlenberg, 2000; Marsiglio & Roy, 2012). Recent qualitative research has begun to uncover deeper and more nuanced understandings of the myriad roles of fatherhood. Fathers, including those who are low-income, talk about their roles in multifaceted ways, spanning provider, teacher, protector, disciplinarian, caretaker, supporter, and coparent functions (Olmstead, Futris, & Pasley, 2009; Summers, Boller, Schiffman, & Raikes, 2006). Becoming a father is also often viewed as the most transformative event in men's lives (Palkovitz, Copes, & Woolfolk, 2001) and increases their awareness of others and changes their orientations of values, goals, and priorities (Daly, Ashbourne, & Brown, 2009). The value men ascribe to the role of fatherhood also positively affects their level of involvement with children (Goldberg, 2011).

There is much to learn about how fatherhood affects men's development and identity in early adulthood. There is no clear portrait of how fatherhood might prompt struggle and growth in the psychological, social, and economic changes typically associated with the transition to adulthood. Relatively little is known about lower income White and Latino fathers (compared to African American fathers), especially for those who live in small- or mid-sized American communities (compared to those who live in major metropolitan areas).

Latino men face a unique set of challenges related to cultural values: the value of *familismo* (familial ideals) may facilitate fathers' connections to their children, but the heavy emphasis on *machismo* (masculine ideals) may undermine these connections. Latino fathers who craft a "hybrid" (or bicultural) style of parenting are more likely to be involved and nurturing fathers and have higher quality father–child and father–mother relationships (Cabrera & Bradley, 2012; see also Cruz et al., 2011; D'Angelo, Palacios, & Chase-Lansdale, 2012). Additionally, undocumented Latino fathers encounter barriers that prevent their involvement in children's lives, including being hesitant to attend school functions because they feel unwelcome, are unfamiliar with the language, and fear deportation (Cabrera, Aldoney, & Tamis-LeMonda, 2013; Jimenez-Castellanos & Gonzalez, 2012).

## Methods

To strengthen the knowledge base, we conducted an exploratory study to probe these issues with men from these communities. Their perspectives are largely missing from research and policy discussions in the United States. This study permits a valuable comparison between two groups of fathers who likely face unique challenges because of race or ethnicity, but common challenges because they have limited resources and parent in the same locales.

**Sample.** We wanted to focus on (a) fathers still parenting young children but who have also had enough time to reflect on their experiences, (b) fathers who are parenting in low-income settings, and (c) Latino and White fathers in these circumstances. We recruited a sample of fathers who had at least one elementary school–aged child from the schools that had the highest percentage of students with free or reduced lunch status and that contained the highest percentage of ESL-Spanish students.

A total of 48 fathers (27 Latino and 21 White) were sampled from two communities in Oregon. Of these, 23 came from a rural town with a population of around 8,000 (35% Hispanic or Latino, 59% White), a median household income of about $46,000, and 18% living in poverty (U.S. Bureau of the Census, 2012). Twenty-five fathers came from a mid-sized city with a population of about 155,000 (20% Hispanic or Latino, 71% White), a median household income of about $44,000, and 17% living in poverty (U.S. Bureau of the Census, 2012).

We chose one elementary school from each of these communities to build a sample for this project. These elementary schools are dual immersion institutions where about half of the study body is Hispanic or Latino, and the majority receives free or reduced lunch. Oregon State University, as a land-grant institution, has longstanding connections to many communities through its Extension division. These connections were particularly important in recruiting Latino fathers, for whom trust and familiarity are important conditions of participation. The principals of each school were responsible for distributing an open invitation letter in all student mailboxes. A phone number and an email address were provided for interested fathers, for whom we then verified eligibility. Participants were provided $25 as a token of appreciation for their involvement.

Although this sampling strategy did not guarantee that all of these men were themselves low-income, they were all men who father in low-income settings. Participants ranged in age from 24 to 56, with a mean age of 42 for White fathers and 36 for Latino fathers. White fathers had been fathers for an average of about 13 years, first becoming fathers at an average age of about 28; for Latino fathers, these figures are 10 and 25. All but one of the fathers was currently married (one Latino father is a widower). Most participants in both groups had two or three children living at home, with the range being from zero to six. The average age of children living at home was just under eight (8.5 for White fathers and 6.9 for Latino). We did not collect background information on fathers' immigration or prior marital statuses, so we cannot say with certainty whether children not living at home were from previous relationships, if they are "adult" children who have left home, or if they are children who did not immigrate with fathers.

Both groups of fathers work an average of 42 hours per week (42.5 for White fathers and 41.4 for Latino), yet the standard deviation was very large for Latino fathers (21.9 versus 6.1), reflecting the irregularity of work for some and extraordinarily long hours for others. White fathers had a significantly higher annual household income than Latino fathers (an average of $40,000–$44,999 versus $20,000–$24,999), but the variability among White fathers was also greater than for Latino fathers. Seventeen participants received some form of government assistance, with the majority (12) being White fathers. Latino fathers primarily worked manual labor jobs in agriculture, the lumber industry, warehouses and factories, and construction; a few Latino fathers had supervisory roles in these settings. White fathers worked a wider range of jobs in construction, sales, service, education, and technology.

**Focus Groups.** This study used in-depth qualitative data gathered in eight focus groups. Focus groups are particularly effective for conducting research with disadvantaged groups. They promote comfort and intimacy while minimizing researcher control and any intimidation respondents may feel (Denzin & Lincoln, 2003; Madriz, 2003; Umaña-Taylor & Bámaca, 2004). Focus groups also stimulate the spontaneous sharing of experiences (Stewart, Shamdasani, & Rook, 2007). They run the risk, however, of being too influenced by the synergy of the group or its most vocal members. But skilled moderators, like those we hired for this project, are able to draw out dissenting opinions and capitalize on these differences to foster healthy discussion and bring visibility to a spectrum of views. Focus groups are especially helpful methods in cases like ours, where one is trying to understand something that is not well known or generate new perspectives (Morgan, 1996). Our aim was not to seek a "representative" sample, but instead to probe the perceptions of fathers who have not been central in research and to aid the development of theories, concepts, and hypotheses.

Each focus group consisted of between 4 and 12 fathers and lasted about 90 minutes. Focus groups were conducted at the schools and led by trained facilitators (Spanish speaking for Latino groups and English speaking for White groups). A member of our research team was also present to track the conversation, make observations, and administer a one-page survey on the background characteristics of participants.

Each focus group was conducted with a common semistructured interview guide. The guide was first developed in English and then translated into Spanish by a Latina member of our research team, after which point we asked several bicultural and bilingual informants to provide feedback on language and cultural relevance. The interview guide probed a range of questions about the meanings and experiences of fatherhood. In this chapter, we draw especially on questions about how fatherhood has had positive and negative effects on psychological well-being, physical health, social relationships, work life, time, and money.

**Analyses.** All sessions were audio recorded and transcribed. Notes taken by the session observer allowed us to assign voices to names, which were later given pseudonyms. A bilingual member of our research team whose native language is Spanish translated the Spanish transcripts. Transcripts were then coded in multiple phases by the researchers, starting with codes to reflect large sections of the interview guide or broad themes (e.g., "effects of fatherhood") and then building codes to reflect specific topics (e.g., "psychological issues," "physical health," "education," "work," "money," "relationship with spouse/partner," and "relationships with friends"). Codes were developed by the research team, applied by the second and third authors, and then crosschecked by the team to ensure reliability. Because we were analyzing eight transcripts, these codes were largely helpful in ensuring that we captured all relevant text related to three emergent themes to which we now turn.

NEW DIRECTIONS FOR CHILD AND ADOLESCENT DEVELOPMENT • DOI: 10.1002/cad

## How Fatherhood Brings Struggle and Growth in Early Adulthood

Three themes were identified in analyses of young men's development in early adulthood. They include (1) contradictions of the good provider and involved father, (2) turning points in identity and life's meanings, and (3) shifting investments in social relationships.

**Contradictions of the Good Provider and Involved Father.** Securing attachment to the labor force is central to both the process of becoming an adult and the provider obligations of fatherhood. This task is particularly challenging for men from low-income and working-class backgrounds, as noted earlier. The work-related responsibilities these men carry, and are expected to carry, they say, bring significant strain. Fathers talked in pointed, and even painful, ways about their struggle to find time for children in the face of their work responsibilities, and about their hope to be better fathers than their fathers were. But they accepted the responsibilities of the provider role as central to their identities as men and fathers—and therefore as adults.

Men must make difficult choices about employment, as better wages and benefits often come with increased responsibilities and hours—and therefore take more time away from children and wives. In having the responsibility to provide for their families, these men sought to strengthen their connection to the labor market and strive for success at work—which further reinforced the need to achieve this central task of adulthood. Roger (White, age 37 years, father of 8 years) talked about making the choice to find more stable employment that would bring benefits for his family:

> I was working in a job with no health benefits, no retirement, anything like that, and when I got married I thought, "This isn't going to work. You know if I get injured or something on the job in ten years, I'm not going to have anything to fall back on," and so made a career change to something that had more security, more insurance. . . . Well not *more* insurance; [just *having*] insurance . . . [I] didn't want to be stuck.

And yet the footing of these fathers in the workforce is also fragile, given the manual labor or service-sector jobs they hold and the limited capital they have as workers. The low-wage work of these fathers also means they have little, if any, control over their schedules. Latino fathers worked particularly long hours—as many as 12–16 hours a day, and sometimes days or weeks away in exhausting physical labor, often in agriculture. They talked of laboring in these ways for many years, with the hope of eventually finding better work. Francisco (Latino, age 29 years, father of 6 years) discussed the pressures of seasonal employment, an experience shared by many Latino fathers in our study:

[T]he problems from our job affects us in not being good fathers. One of the main things here in the United States is the job ... wherever you go there is always a season. Here in Oregon, the irrigation season is beginning, when the irrigation season is ending, then the harvesting come on us, and after the harvest come the pine trees, and after the pine trees the trimming and there it all ends. And then the irrigation begins again. Then in each process, in each season of three months you will be happy, and you are trying to think in being a good father. But it will end and then you are terminated ... then you are not going to be good father. Because you don't think about your children or about your wife. You are thinking all the time about the bills.

Men recognized the need for stable employment, but they also found it burdensome and threatening to simultaneous expectations related to father involvement. They pressed on as providers because of their children and wives, but they did so with a sharp and often aching awareness of the toll that the provider role takes on their family relationships. Tom (White, age 30 years, father of 6 years) illustrated the struggle to balance work and family:

Being a good father is about presence.... Even if you're at home working, or if you're at the office working, you're not there, you're absentee.... What ball do you drop, you know? ... When I start catching myself dropping the family ball, it really hurts. But if I drop the work ball ... we don't eat. So I'm always stuck trying to keep all those balls in the air.

Unlike Latino fathers, White fathers' struggles were more often construed as *choices to be made* rather than *circumstances to be endured*. Within this context, White fathers referenced the "deathbed" story—asking who among them would ever look back on their lives thinking "Gee, I wish I'd worked more," and who among them will regret having spent too little time with their families. A variant of this story was raised in every group of White fathers, as if it has been rehearsed in advanced and repeated as a mantra to keep in perspective the significance of these decisions.

The challenge, according to fathers, is to be aware of personal priorities and make choices that ultimately put the family first. This is, of course, easier to do when fathers have choices—or at least *perceive* that they have choices. Latino fathers seemed to feel more trapped in work that only allowed them to be providers. White fathers seemed more often to have bosses or work environments that were more accommodating of family needs, though they did say that this put them at a disadvantage for opportunities related to better pay or possible advancement. This may fuel their greater sense that there are choices to be made. Latino fathers, in contrast, often did not have this luxury: they said that if they took time off from work for any reason, they risked losing their jobs, not pay or promotions.

For fathers of both groups, being a provider was not viewed as being enough for their children or for the men themselves. In this way, these fathers sounded remarkably like more privileged fathers. They wanted to give their children more than they had growing up, but it meant that time with children would be compromised. Gustavo's (Latino, age 45 years, father of 14 years) emotional recollection is particularly poignant. Choking up, he told a story of giving his son money to buy a soccer ball he desperately wanted, only to be told, "You know, Dad, why would I want a ball if you don't play with me?" The struggle between being a provider and fulfilling more nurturing roles is one that these fathers often felt they could not win, given their work constraints and limited resources, and left them close to a "breaking point," as several men noted, with the stress they carry and the sleep they lose. So, while being a father may help solidify productive paths into adulthood through work, the tensions they already felt as disadvantaged men were only heightened by fatherhood.

**Turning Points in Identity and Life's Meanings.** Consistent with the idea that becoming adult entails becoming interdependent with rather than independent from others, men in our focus groups emphasized that once they became fathers, they were no longer simply responsible for themselves, as their decisions and actions affected the children and partners who depend on them. Even more, these men said, fatherhood provoked fundamental changes in their identities—who they were before fatherhood was remarkably different from who they became after fatherhood—and the gains far outweighed what was lost. These gains were largely about meaning, purpose, and fulfillment. Children also forced men to set and constantly reevaluate priorities, and to put into perspective their own personal troubles. In short, for both groups of men, fatherhood became a central dimension for organizing their identity. Ruperto (Latino, age 24 years, father of 8 years) is a typical example of how fathering became a positive turning point in the lives of these men:

> I think my life has changed through the lives of my children. Before, every-
> thing was easy to me, but since they came is very different from a bachelor to
> a married man ... You stop going out, you stop to give them education, first
> is to be with them more than with other people and to know how to educate
> them, know to take care for them, know to love them, for me that made me
> change everything.

Similarly, Alan (White, age 38 years, father of 9 years) shared:

> I mean, yeah, the kids are, they're kind of part of who I am ... I'm a father
> you know, I've got a job and ... I'm doing different things and that's also part
> of me, but you know being a father is who I am, and I actually don't imagine
> having ... my life without my kids anymore.

Several fathers were quick to point out that their lives were headed in destructive directions before they married and had children. This was especially true for Latino fathers, who emphasized that their children and wives kept them "in check" and away from risky behavior and people. Seferino (Latino, age 34 years, father of 5 years) is a good example:

> [T]he truth is I did not know how to be a father, but I did it in the end. And now I have 3 children because as [the other participant] said, you change ... being with the family, the wife there, going out with them to have fun in the park, and [you feel] more comfortable with it. I do not go out with friends because we get wasted sometimes and today I live for the family, before [it was] for the friends ... the family changes you.

Lurking in the stress of fatherhood is the potential for personal growth. The tasks of nurturing and caretaking, and the raw daily emotions that come with parenting, men said, can prompt self-reflection and teach lessons about love, patience, and self-control. Latino men more often expressed concerns about how to achieve these things because of the perceived need to reject some of the practices of their own parents and country of origin if they were to be successful fathers. A few Latino fathers suggested that aspects of Latino culture were problematic for couples—that they were not intentional enough about family planning (they should more carefully plan the number and timing of children), and that the division of labor between mothers and fathers was too rigid and gendered (with women too exclusively bound to family responsibilities and men to economic ones). Several of these men said they felt constrained by these expectations and wanted to be more involved as fathers and grow as men. As Cecilio (Latino, age 27 years, father of 9 years) said:

> One of the things we should ... realize and begin to accept when we live with a partner, is the culture, want it or not, [that] we were educated, born and grew up in [is] a patriarchal society where the father, the man, has certain roles, responsibility that [he] must assume as a man. And the same patriarchal society also gives roles to women who have to assume and accept them, like it or not. ... And this [is] true for me personally, [it] is one of the things I have been always fighting internally, with myself. ... In the end, we both carry the pants in the house. ... I always talk with my wife about it. [When] ... we had our children, I started to face all my fears [that he would give in to these expected gender roles]. That's how I grew up and this is how I learned, but it's not like I want to be. ... The two [parents] have a responsibility to raise this life ... and take on tasks that must be focused on our children, not on "that's your turn now" as ... my culture says.

For both groups, the ultimate message was clear: fatherhood encourages—or implores—them to be better men.

NEW DIRECTIONS FOR CHILD AND ADOLESCENT DEVELOPMENT • DOI: 10.1002/cad

**Shifting Investments in Social Relationships.** Building a lasting intimate relationship is a central task of adulthood, and having a good relationship with one's wife was seen as the biggest key to being a good father and coparent. This, fathers said, rests on strong communication and the need to model a healthy relationship for children. But as fathers talked about the pressures of providing for their families and finding the time and energy to be involved with their children, they also said that it was their marriages that ultimately paid the price, as couples had limited time together and the strains of parenting interfered with their relationship.

Latino and White fathers alike emphasized that wives were an important source of emotional support. As Francisco (Latino, age 29 years, father of 6 years) notes, "[W]hen I return home ... everyday I get more motivated by myself and my wife, talking to her, because she is my companion, my other half and therefore I trust her ... and my mood is up because of her." For Francisco and many other men, wives and children provided emotional support that motivated them to endure the hardships and stress of their jobs. Additionally, wives provided men with instrumental support that helped them be better fathers, with multiple men even referring to their wives as "coaches." Take Pete (White, age 46 years, father of 10 years), for example:

> I'm going to use the word "coach" in my situation. She's ... on the sidelines watching the game, you know, the kids going against dad, dad going against the kids, and then she's there for those helpful pointers on ... "You could probably get what you want done if you try this or try that," and it's an adult objective, common values, 'cause that's why you selected her in the first place, and you know she's trying to raise these kids too.

Many fathers talked about how they formed a "unified front" with their wives when addressing their children, but consulted with each other in private, especially for his benefit.

The premium on family time led men to also report that fatherhood both restricted time with friends and demanded that they make better choices about friends. Often at the insistence of wives, men recognized that some friendships were unhealthy and unsupportive in their roles as fathers. This prompted the need or desire for new friendships with other parents, especially those with children of similar ages. Relationships with childless friends fell away, whether by choice or circumstance. Being a father, then, led to the creation of healthier ties that fostered a more stable daily existence and reinforced their commitments to productive work roles and family relationships.

Latino fathers, especially, reported that friends were once a negative influence in their lives, but that wives and children had since become protective factors. Latino men were quick to credit their wives for encouraging them to stop self-destructive behaviors (especially alcohol or drug use, or hanging out with friends who engaged in risky behavior), and they saw the presence of wives and children as strong forces that kept them on the "straight and narrow."

White fathers, in contrast, more often mourned the close single friends they had to leave behind after they married and had children, not because the friends were a negative influence but because their lifestyles no longer meshed with the expectations and rhythms of family life. The friendships men reported having as fathers were healthier and deeper than when they were single, but they still had little time to devote to them, and social activities, like playing sports, got harder to schedule or were not worth the money or the time lost with family.

Apart from wives, men emphasized the importance of extended family members. Fatherhood, they said, enhanced or restored relationships with a wide range of family members who provided emotional and instrumental support. Latino fathers stressed the significance of family relationships in their culture and talked about how living apart from family posed significant social and economic hardships. White men also noted the importance of extended family relationships, but in comparison to Latino men they referenced a much narrower set of relationships—mainly parents and siblings—and they more often lamented the fact that these relationships had to be maintained from a distance rather than that the well-being of their family depended on these relationships.

## Discussion and Conclusion

The fathers in our study have provided insight into how fatherhood, which has long been considered a traditional marker of the transition to adulthood, matters for men's development in early adulthood. We have focused on two groups of disadvantaged men who have often been invisible in research and policy: predominantly low-income White and Latino men in small- and mid-sized American communities. Because of their ages, and because the transition to both adulthood and fatherhood are long-term processes, these men were well positioned to reflect on their experiences. Indeed, like so many life experiences, it is only in having spent some time in this process that men felt they had accumulated enough experience and perspective to derive these insights.

Their insights lead to a bold and resounding message: that despite—and even because of—their struggles to meet the claims of both provider and involved father, fatherhood facilitates other social and economic roles, as well as personal capacities, that are typically expected as men move into adulthood. These processes are interrelated. From their struggle comes a deeper connection and commitment to the labor market, psychological growth and a greater sense of purpose and meaning, and stronger relationships with wives and extended family members and friends. For these men, fatherhood complicates and exacerbates their already significant challenges. But the resolution, if largely successful, can also strengthen attachment to productive roles and relationships—and bring the awareness that ties that bind also bring opportunities, reinforcing the notion introduced earlier that interdependence, rather than independence, may be the hallmark of adult life.

The care and concern that these fathers expressed for their families, and especially their children, underscores the need for fathers, in all their complexity, to be a stronger part of the child and family policy agenda (for an excellent discussion, see Marsiglio & Roy, 2012). The many good things that fathers like these provide are somehow out of the public eye. The experiences of these men make a strong case for moving the conversation away from deficiency-based models of vulnerable fathers and toward strength-based models—models that acknowledge not only their serious challenges but also their significant capacities and responsibilities in becoming and being better fathers. This is especially revealed in their perseverance in finding jobs that allow them to be good providers to their families and also to be present for their wives and children. Being the financial provider is simply not enough for these men. They want much more out of their family lives and are striving to make decisions and acquire resources that will allow them to be more involved. In this way, their struggles sound remarkably like those of working women and middle-class men who are wrestling with the balance between work and family.

A large body of evidence suggests that the strongest pathway into adulthood is one in which marriage and, especially, parenthood are actively postponed so that young people can concentrate on making investments in their human capital, especially higher education (see Settersten, 2012). Indeed, the normative model is now one in which parenting culminates the process of becoming adult, which naturally leads to concerns about the potential negative outcomes that come to those who parent early, should it cut short their educational attainment or leave them in more precarious employment that offers low wages, few benefits, and little mobility. Here, too, there is ample evidence, for women and men alike, of the real risks of moving too quickly into parenting. There is, however, a persistent question of whether it is early parenthood that causes these negative outcomes, or whether it is other existing disadvantages that causes early parenting (Furstenberg, 2007).

While these men highlight the important positive effects that fatherhood brings to their lives, this is not to say that fatherhood is the solution to improving the lives of disadvantaged men. To the contrary, the occurrence of fatherhood brings extraordinary challenges for men and for the women and children involved. Fatherhood is clearly not an experience to be taken lightly. It is simply to say that, in shining a spotlight on how fatherhood affects men, this and other emerging research suggests that fatherhood can prompt developmental gains alongside its strains and compromises. It is

NEW DIRECTIONS FOR CHILD AND ADOLESCENT DEVELOPMENT • DOI: 10.1002/cad

also important to note that these gains are not likely to result from simply being a father, but instead from being an *involved* father.

Although low-income Latino and White fathers share many of the same struggles, White fathers have more choices—or at least have this perception. Nevertheless, both groups see fatherhood as being about hard choices. Investing in fatherhood necessarily comes with serious demands and compromises in work and family life, and for most of these fathers, this battle is one they often feel they cannot win. Being the ideal father—a great provider and fully involved with children—seems a privilege that few men can attain. Fathers are expected to provide for their family, but not at the cost of being disengaged fathers. To live up to this ideal, fathers must have the resources to work a job that not only provides sufficient resources for their families but also offers enough flexibility to spend time with family.

Planning is a core tenet in scholarship and policy-making related to the transition to adulthood (for a discussion, see Hallevik & Settersten, 2012). The assumption is that careful planning in young adulthood comes with better outcomes—and it generally does. However, careful planning is more possible for people whose lives are predictable and who have resources that allow them to do so. Young people from middle-class backgrounds are taught to plan ahead and can assume a set of resources that promote their development and opportunities. This is not the case for the men in our study. For these men, fatherhood is a source of meaning and fulfillment in a world that often feels as if it does not do right by them—a theme that parallels Edin and Kefalas's (2005) study of low-income mothers. If the future seems foreclosed, these men may have few incentives to delay fatherhood, especially if they imagine it to bring some of the benefits they claim. This notion assumes a level of intentionality related to fertility that may not be reflected in reality.

These findings also pose a challenge to policies that problematize these types of men. An exclusive focus on family planning as an intervention strategy may not be an effective route to altering the fertility behavior of these men, especially Latino men for whom early fertility is part of their culture. Rather, if parenthood offers some potential positive outcomes for this population, it will be more effective to craft policies that support and resource men in their roles as fathers in order to ensure these outcomes. Involved fathering becomes the mechanism (or, the "evoker," to use Palkovitz et al.'s [2001] term) that likely brings about these effects. It might also be a mechanism for better incorporating at-risk men, including Latino men, into society through their involvement in mainstream social institutions, such as schools. At the same time, there are clearly risks associated with early fertility, whether in limiting opportunities in education and work, the viability of partnerships or marriages, or the personal and social resources one can bring to parenting.

Policy strategies should not only focus on minimizing the risks and challenges associated with fatherhood, but also on maximizing its potentials. We have seen that fatherhood can serve as a gateway to adult development for disadvantaged men—as an anchor for productive roles and relationships, and as a mechanism for building social integration and social capital, all of which can compensate for some of the vulnerabilities these men may have in other realms of life. In these ways, fatherhood becomes a kind of desistance from risk (see also Kerr et al., 2011; Sampson & Laub, 2005). One begins to wonder what additional potentials might be gotten from fatherhood if the resources of these men were strengthened.

Finally, several shortcomings of this project should be emphasized. Our restricted sample and focus-group methods have generated important insights that should be examined with larger samples, other populations, and other modes of measurement. The men who participated were probably also drawn to the study because they are already committed fathers and, seemingly, committed husbands. The lessons learned were therefore about fathers and husbands who, despite their struggles, are managing to make it in these roles. Given the support that these men receive in their relationships, their stories, however hard, may pale in comparison to men who have troubled or broken relationships, or who became fathers as teenagers. At the same time, many of the themes we have described may be widely shared among committed fathers in other socioeconomic statuses, races and ethnicities, and locations—and at a time when meeting the expectations of the ideal father has become more difficult, and when the stakes for both men and their families have gotten bigger.

## References

Arnett, J. J. (2000). Emerging adulthood: A theory of development from the late teens through the twenties. *American Psychologist, 55*(5), 469–480.

Astone, N. M., Dariotis, J., Sonenstein, F., Pleck, J. H., & Hynes, K. (2010). Men's work efforts and the transition to fatherhood. *Journal of Family Economic Issues, 31*(1), 3–13.

Cabrera, N. J., Aldoney, D., & Tamis-LeMonda, C. S. (2013). Latino fathers. In N. J. Cabrera & C. S. Tamis-LeMonda (Eds.), *Handbook of father involvement: Multidisciplinary perspectives* (pp. 244–260). New York, NY: Taylor & Francis.

Cabrera, N. J., & Bradley, R. H. (2012). Latino fathers and their children. *Child Development Perspectives, 6*(3), 232–238.

Cherlin, A. J. (2010). Demographic trends in the United States: A review of research in the 2000s. *Journal of Marriage and Family, 72*, 403–419.

Côté, J. E. (2000). *Arrested adulthood: The changing nature of maturity and identity.* New York: New York University Press.

Cruz, R. A., King, K. M., Widaman, K. F., Leu, J., Cauce, A. M., & Conger, R. D. (2011). Cultural influences on positive father involvement in two-parent Mexican-origin families. *Journal of Family Psychology, 25*(5), 731–740.

Daly, K. J., Ashbourne, L., & Brown, J. L. (2009). Fathers' perceptions of children's influence: Implications for involvement. *The Annals of the American Academy of Political and Social Science, 624*, 61–77.

D'Angelo, A. V., Palacios, N. A., & Chase-Lansdale, P. L. (2012). Latino immigrant differences in father involvement with infants. *Fathering, 10*(2), 178–212.

Dariotis, J. K., Pleck, J. H., Astone, N. M., & Sonenstein, F. L. (2011). Pathways of early fatherhood, marriage, and employment: A latent class growth analysis. *Demography*, 48, 593–623.

Denzin, N. K., & Lincoln, Y. S. (Eds.). (2003). *Collecting and interpreting qualitative materials* (2nd ed.). Thousand Oaks, CA: Sage.

Dew, J., & Eggebeen, D. J. (2010). Beyond the wage premium: Fatherhood and asset accumulation. *Research in Human Development*, 7(2), 140–158.

Duckworth, J. D., & Buzzanell, P. M. (2009). Constructing work-life balance and fatherhood: Men's framing of the meanings of both work and family. *Communication Studies*, 60(5), 558–573.

Edin, K., & Kefalas, M. (2005). *Promises I can keep: Why poor women put motherhood before marriage*. Berkeley: University of California Press.

Eggebeen, D. J., Knoester, C., & McDaniel, B. (2013). The implications of fatherhood for men. In N. J. Cabrera & C. S. Tamis-LeMonda (Eds.), *Handbook of father involvement: Multidisciplinary perspectives* (pp. 338–358). New York, NY: Taylor & Francis.

Furstenberg, F. F., Jr. (2007). *Destinies of the disadvantaged: The politics of teenage childbearing*. New York, NY: Russell Sage Foundation.

Furstenberg, F. F., Jr. (2010). On a new schedule: Transitions to adulthood and family change. *The Future of Children*, 20(1), 67–87.

Goldberg, J. S. (2011). *Identity salience and involvement among resident and nonresident fathers* (CDE Working Paper No. 2011-06). Madison, WI: Center for Demography and Ecology. Retrieved from http://www.ssc.wisc.edu/cde/cdewp/2011-06.pdf

Goldscheider, F., Hofferth, S., Spearin, C., & Curtin, S. (2009). Fatherhood across two generations: Factors affecting early family roles. *Journal of Family Issues*, 30, 586–604.

Hallevik, T., & Settersten, R. A., Jr. (2012). Life planning among young adults in 23 European countries: The effects of individual and country security. *European Sociological Review*, 29(5), 923–938. doi:10.1093/esr/jcs069

Hofferth, S. L., & Goldscheider, F. (2010). Family structure and the transition to early parenthood. *Demography*, 47(2), 415–437.

Jimenez-Castellanos, O., & Gonzalez, G. (2012). Understanding the impact of microaggressions on engagement of undocumented Latino immigrant fathers: Debunking deficit thinking. *Journal of Latinos and Education*, 11, 204–217.

Kaufman, G., & Uhlenberg, P. (2000). The influence of parenthood on the work effort of married men and women. *Social Forces*, 78(3), 931–947.

Kerr, D. C. R., Capaldi, D. M., Owen, L. D., Wiesner, M., & Pears, K. C. (2011). Changes in at-risk American men's crime and substance use trajectories following fatherhood. *Journal of Marriage and Family*, 73(5), 1101–1116.

Madriz, E. (2003). Focus groups in feminist research. In N. K. Denzin & Y. S. Lincoln (Eds.), *Collecting and interpreting qualitative materials* (2nd ed., pp. 364–388). Thousand Oaks, CA: Sage.

Marsiglio, W., & Roy, K. (2012). *Nurturing dads: Social initiatives for contemporary fatherhood*. New York, NY: Russell Sage Foundation.

Morgan, D. L. (1996). Focus groups. *Annual Review of Sociology*, 22, 129–152.

Olmstead, S. B., Futris, T. G., & Pasley, K. (2009). An exploration of married and divorced, nonresident men's perceptions and organization of their father role identity. *Fathering*, 7(3), 249–268.

Palkovitz, R., Copes, M. A., & Woolfolk, T. N. (2001). "It's like . . . you discover a new sense of being": Involved fathering as an evoker of adult development. *Men and Masculinities*, 4, 46–69.

Palkovitz, R., & Palm, G. (2009). Transitions within fathering. *Fathering*, 7(1), 3–22.

Pears, K. C., Pierce, S. L., Kim, H. K., Capaldi, D. M., & Owen, L. D. (2005). The timing of entry into fatherhood in young at-risk men. *Journal of Marriage and Family*, 67(2), 429–447.

Roy, K., Vesely, C., Fitzgerald, M., & Buckmiller Jones, N. (2010). Young fathers at work: The influence of parental closeness and contact on employment. *Research in Human Development*, 7(2), 123–129.

Sampson, R. J., & Laub, J. H. (2005). A life-course view of the development of crime. *The Annals of the American Academy of Political and Social Science*, 602, 12–45.

Settersten, R. A., Jr. (2011). Becoming adult: Meanings and markers for young Americans. In M. Waters, P. Carr, M. Kefalas, & J. Holdaway (Eds.), *Coming of age in America* (pp. 169–190). Berkeley: University of California Press.

Settersten, R. A., Jr. (2012). The contemporary context of young adulthood in the United States. In A. Booth, S. Brown, N. Landale, S. McHale, & W. Manning (Eds.), *Early adulthood in a family context* (pp. 3–26). New York, NY: Springer.

Settersten, R. A., Jr., & Cancel-Tirado, D. (2010). Fatherhood as a hidden variable in men's development and life courses. *Research in Human Development*, 7(2), 83–102.

Settersten, R. A., Jr., Furstenberg, F. F., Jr., & Rumbaut, R. G. (Eds.). (2005). *On the frontier of adulthood: Theory, research, and public policy*. Chicago, IL: University of Chicago Press.

Settersten R. A., Jr., & Ray, B. (2010). What's going on with young people today? The long and twisting path to adulthood. *The Future of Children*, 20(1), 19–41.

Spéder, Z., Murinkó, L., & Settersten, R. A., Jr. (2014). Are conceptions of adulthood universal and unisex? Ages and social markers in 25 European countries. *Social Forces*, 92(3), 873–898.

Stewart, D. W., Shamdasani, P. N., & Rook, D. W. (2007). *Focus groups: Theory and practice* (2nd ed.). Thousand Oaks, CA: Sage.

Summers, J. A., Boller, K., Schiffman, R. F., & Raikes, H. H. (2006). The meaning of "good fatherhood": Low-income fathers' social constructions of their roles. *Parenting: Science and Practice*, 6(2–3), 145–165.

Umaña-Taylor, A., & Bámaca, M. (2004). Conducting focus groups with Latino populations: Lessons from the field. *Family Relations*, 53(3), 261–272.

U.S. Bureau of the Census. (2012). *Quickfacts from the 2010 Census*. Retrieved from http://quickfacts.census.gov/qfd/

RICHARD A. SETTERSTEN, JR., *is endowed director of the Hallie E. Ford Center for Healthy Children & Families and a professor of human development and family sciences at Oregon State University. E-mail: richard.settersten@oregonstate.edu*

JACK K. DAY *is a doctoral candidate in human development and family sciences at Oregon State University.*

DORIS CANCEL-TIRADO *is an assistant professor of community health at Western Oregon University.*

DEBRA MINAR DRISCOLL *is a professor of family and community health with the Oregon State University Extension Service.*

NEW DIRECTIONS FOR CHILD AND ADOLESCENT DEVELOPMENT • DOI: 10.1002/cad

# Index

co-participating in an organized activity with your friend improve the quality of the relationship; (2) When do peer relations amplify the benefits of participating and when do they exacerbate negative outcomes; and (3) Does participation in organized activities help adolescents manage difficult transition periods? Finally, the volume concludes with a conceptual framework to guide future research on how organized activity characteristics influence peer processes and how these processes within organized activity contexts influence outcomes for adolescents.
*ISBN 978-11187-35756*

CAD139   **Digital Games: A Context for Cognitive Development**
*Fran C. Blumberg, Shalom M. Fisch, Editors*
In the United States and in many other countries around the world, digital games have become an integral part of children's lives. Discussions of research on youth and digital games often focus solely on negative effects (e.g., of violent video games), but this is far from the whole story. As natural problem-solving activities, digital games provide a rich context for applied cognition. This volume explores topics such as the benefits of digital games for children and adolescents' cognitive skills, the nature of their learning from educational media, the influence of developmental factors on their interactions with digital games, and the use of developmental research and established educational practice to create effective educational games that they will play.
*ISBN 978-11186-41019*

CAD138   **Identity Around the World**
*Seth J. Schwartz, Editor*
This volume examines the structure and context of identity development in a number of different countries: Belgium, The Netherlands, Germany, Sweden, Italy, China, and Japan. Although Erikson believed that identity development proceeded in much the same way across national contexts, the chapters in this volume suggest that there are important nuances in the ways in which identity unfolds in each country. Macrocultural forces, such as permissiveness in Sweden, collective guilt in Germany, and filial piety in China, direct the identity development process in important ways. Expectations regarding obligations and ties to family also direct the identity development process differently in many of the countries included in this volume—such as extended co-residence with parents in Italy, lifelong obligations to follow parents' wishes in China, and democratic independence in Sweden. The various countries are compared and contrasted against the United States, where much of the early identity research was conducted. The volume also reviews specific identity challenges facing immigrant and ethnic-minority individuals in countries that receive large numbers of immigrants—Germany, Sweden, Belgium, The Netherlands, and Italy—and suggests many future directions for identity research in various parts of the world.
*ISBN 978-11185-44112*

CAD137    ***Applications of Dialogical Self Theory***
          *Hubert J. M. Hermans, Editor*
          In a globalizing society, in which individuals, groups, and cultures are
          increasingly interconnected, a dialogical self is not only possible but even
          necessary. In a hyperconnected world, people are closer together than ever
          in the history of humanity, yet they are confronted with apparent and
          sometimes even insurmountable differences. At the heart of this volume is
          the thought that the simultaneity of interdependence and difference needs
          not only the development of dialogue *between* individuals, groups, and
          cultures, but also the development of the dialogical potentials *within* the self
          of the individual person. Elaborating on these concerns, the authors of this
          volume present and discuss a Dialogical Self Theory based on the
          assumption that the self functions as a *society of mind*. The self is not simply
          participating in a "surrounding" society, but functions itself as a
          mini-society, which is, at the same time, part of the society at large. The
          authors present the theory in detail, explore the developmental origins of
          the dialogical self, and elaborate on the identity development of adolescents
          growing up in multicultural societies, with attention to the experience of
          uncertainty and identity confusion. Finally, a striking example of a social
          movement in India is discussed, showing how individual and collective
          voices merge in a nationwide protest.
          *ISBN 978-11184-45136*

CAD136    ***Independent Child Migration—Insights into Agency, Vulnerability, and***
          ***Structure***
          *Aida Orgocka, Christina Clark-Kazak, Editors*
          This volume contributes to a growing body of literature on international
          independent child migration. It gives particular focus to agency and
          vulnerability as central concepts for understanding the diverse experiences
          of children who have migrated alone. These concepts provide theoretical
          and empirical insights into the complexity of children's experiences.
          Combining perspectives from academics and practitioners, the volume
          challenges readers to critically assess the categorization processes related to
          both migration and childhood that independent child migrants encounter,
          and argues for greater attention to the ways in which categories are
          constructed in theory and practice. Reading this collection will provide
          scholars and practitioners with thought-provoking insights into the nature
          of current programmatic interventions for independent child migrants. It
          further invites researchers, practitioners, and policy-makers to critically
          reflect on the complex socio-economic, political, and cultural contexts in
          which migration decisions are taken. Contributors recognize that
          independent child migrants, despite vulnerabilities, are active
          decision-makers in determining movement, responding to violent and
          discriminatory situations, resisting stereotypical assumptions, and figuring
          out integration and life choices as these are shaped by existing structural
          opportunities and constraints.
          *ISBN 978-11183-52823*

CAD135    *Family Conflict Among Chinese- and Mexican-Origin Adolescents and Their Parents in the U.S.*
Linda P. Juang, Adriana J. Umaña-Taylor, Editors
Parentadolescent conflict in immigrant families has long been conceptualized as inevitable due to the inherent stresses of the acculturation process; this volume provides a more nuanced understanding of parent–adolescent conflict in Chinese- and Mexican-origin families in the United States. In their chapters, authors explore key issues related to family conflict such as acculturation gaps, parent and adolescent internal conflicts, conflict resolution, and seeking out confidants for help in coping with conflict. This volume showcases the complexity of conflict among Chinese- and Mexican-origin families and furthers our understanding of how both developmental and cultural sources of parentadolescent conflict are linked to adjustment.
ISBN 978-11183-09117

CAD134    **Youth Civic Development: Work at the Cutting Edge**
*Constance A. Flanagan, Brian D. Christens, Editors*
Civic engagement of young people is increasingly understood as an important feature of democratic functioning in communities, organizations, and societies. It has also become clear that the civic domain is indispensable as a context for understanding human development processes. This volume brings together cutting-edge work from leading scholars in the interdisciplinary field of youth civic development. Their work makes the case for greater consideration of justice, social responsibility, critical consciousness, and collective action in our understanding of child and adolescent development.
The volume proposes the following central theses in relation to youth civic development:
• It is rooted in the realities of young people's everyday lives.
• It is collectively constructed.
• It raises questions about the principles, values, and relationships that bind people together in societies.
• It raises questions about power and justice.
Youth civic development pushes the broader field of child and adolescent development to focus on the social issues with which younger generations are grappling and the identities they are constructing—issues that also are shaped by structural inequalities and by the collective actions of youth. The volume builds on themes of agency and assets from the field of positive youth development and points to ways that the critical analysis and engagement of young people in their society can contribute to social change.
ISBN 978-11182-29217

# NEW DIRECTIONS FOR CHILD AND ADOLESCENT DEVELOPMENT

# ORDER FORM SUBSCRIPTION AND SINGLE ISSUES

## DISCOUNTED BACK ISSUES:

Use this form to receive 20% off all back issues of *New Directions for Child and Adolescent Development*.
All single issues priced at **$23.20** (normally $29.00)

| TITLE | ISSUE NO. | ISBN |
|-------|-----------|------|
| | | |
| | | |

*Call 888-378-2537 or see mailing instructions below. When calling, mention the promotional code JBNND
to receive your discount. For a complete list of issues, please visit www.josseybass.com/go/ndcad*

## SUBSCRIPTIONS: (1 YEAR, 4 ISSUES)

☐ New Order       ☐ Renewal

| | | |
|---|---|---|
| U.S. | ☐ Individual: $89 | ☐ Institutional: $388 |
| CANADA/MEXICO | ☐ Individual: $89 | ☐ Institutional: $428 |
| ALL OTHERS | ☐ Individual: $113 | ☐ Institutional: $462 |

*Call 888-378-2537 or see mailing and pricing instructions below.
Online subscriptions are available at www.onlinelibrary.wiley.com*

## ORDER TOTALS:

Issue / Subscription Amount: $ _____

Shipping Amount: $ _____
*(for single issues only – subscription prices include shipping)*

**Total Amount:** $ _____

SHIPPING CHARGES:

| | |
|---|---|
| First Item | $6.00 |
| Each Add'l Item | $2.00 |

*(No sales tax for U.S. subscriptions. Canadian residents, add GST for subscription orders. Individual rate subscriptions must
be paid by personal check or credit card. Individual rate subscriptions may not be resold as library copies.)*

## BILLING & SHIPPING INFORMATION:

☐ **PAYMENT ENCLOSED:** *(U.S. check or money order only. All payments must be in U.S. dollars.)*

☐ **CREDIT CARD:**   ☐ VISA   ☐ MC   ☐ AMEX

Card number _____Exp. Date_____

Card Holder Name_____Card Issue # _____

Signature _____Day Phone_____

☐ **BILL ME:** *(U.S. institutional orders only. Purchase order required.)*

Purchase order #_____
Federal Tax ID 13559302 • GST 89102-8052

Name_____

Address_____

Phone_____ E-mail_____

Copy or detach page and send to: **John Wiley & Sons, One Montgomery Street, Suite 1200,
San Francisco, CA 94104-4594**

Order Form can also be faxed to: **888-481-2665**

PROMO JBNND

# Stay Informed with Wiley Publications

### The Brown University Child and Adolescent Behavior Letter

12 issues for ~~$199~~ **SAVE 50%!**
$99.50 (print)  $89.50 (electronic)

Stay current with the news, research, clinical studies, and information you need to know in order to diagnose and treat psychiatric, behavioral, and developmental problems. Every issue is filled with practical applications, new therapies, prevention techniques, and research findings on issues seen in children and adolescent patients.

www.childadolescentbehavior.com

### The Brown University Child and Adolescent Psychopharmacology Update

12 issues for ~~$199~~ **SAVE 50%!**
$99.50 (print)  $89.50 (electronic)

The latest news and information on children and adolescents' psychotropic medication—new drugs, new uses, typical doses, side effects, interactions, generic vs. name brand, reports on new research, and new indications for existing medications. Also includes case studies, industry news, abstracts of current research, and patient medication handouts.

www.childadolescentpsychopharm.com

### The Brown University Psychopharmacology Update

12 issues for ~~$199~~ **SAVE 50%!**
$99.50 (print)  $89.50 (electronic)

These psychotropic drug updates help you stay current with the late: therapeutic treatments. You'll get bias-free information on new drug in the pipeline, the latest evidence for a particular drug treatment, a newly discovered side effect, reports on drug interactions, and the latest FDA information.

www.psychopharmacologyupdate.con

---

### New Directions for Youth Development

4 issues for ~~$89~~ **SAVE 15%!** $75.65 (print or electronic)

This acclaimed periodical presents the latest theory, practice and research on youth development. Past topics include youth mentoring, threat and terror, immigrant youth, afterschool time, community building, and youth leadership.

### Alcoholism & Drug Abuse Weekly

48 issues for ~~$695~~ **SAVE 50%!**
$347.50 (print)  $277.50 (electronic)

This weekly delivers all the latest news, trends, opportunities, and efficiencies to improve your quality of treatment—and your bottom line.

ADAW is filled with the latest information on national trends and developments in funding and policy issues, legislation, treatment, prevention, avoiding relapse, and research—anything that affects managing your program and caring for your clients.

www.alcoholismdrugabuseweekly.com

### New Directions for Child and Adolescent Development

4 issues for ~~$89~~ **SAVE 15%!** $75.65 (print or electroni⬤

The latest scholarship from the field of child and adolescent development. Topics include social, cognitive, educational, emotional, biological, and socio-cultural issues that bear on children and youth, as well as issues in research methodology and other domains.

### Mental Health Weekly

48 issues for ~~$699~~ **SAVE 50%!**
$347.50 (print)  $277.50 (electronic)

This premier weekly publication brings you the latest information on fundamental issues, such as practice trends, state funding and policy issues, litigation, federal legislation and policy, workforce news, progra⬤ success stories, and innovative practices—everything you need to stay informed and manage your practice.

www.mentalhealthweeklynews.com

---

## SUBSCRIBE TODAY

Call 888.378.2537. Use promo code PSY14 and get discounted subscription rates—see below.

WILEY